Help, There's a Computer in My Church!

HELP, THERE'S A COMPUTER IN MY CHURCH!

Practical Advice for Using Computers in Ministry

DAVID TRAMMEL

BROADMAN PRESS
NASHVILLE, TENNESSEE

© Copyright 1990 ● Broadman Press
All Rights Reserved
4230-07
ISBN: 0-8054-3007-5
Dewey Decimal Classification: 254
Subject Headings: COMPUTERS
Library of Congress Catalog Number: 90-33439
Printed in the United States of America

Library of Congress Cataloging-in-Publication Data

Trammel, David, 1948-

    Help, there's a computer in my church! / David Trammel.

    p.   cm.

    ISBN 0-8054-3007-5

    1. Church management--Data processing.   I. Title.

BV652.77.T73 1991

254'.00285--dc20

96-1220

90-33439

CIP

This book is dedicated to the sincere hope that computers can become a tool churches use to:
" 'Go out into the highways and along the hedges, and compel them to come in, that my house may be filled' " (Luke 14:23, NASB).

Contents

Preface

This book is about putting computers to use in the church office. It is not a technical manual on hardware or software. While care has been taken to insure technical accuracy, it is entirely possible that while the book is at the printer new developments in the computer industry could change what is technically correct.

Changes in technology will not change the value of this book. It is primarily about using information to further ministry. Computers can usher in a new era in the church's ability to reach out to people. For this era to begin, ministers must begin to think in new ways about managing information. This book introduces possibilities, gives practical suggestions, and, hopefully, challenges the reader to put information to use.

Acknowledgments

My experience in church computer applications began at the First Baptist Church of Norcross, Georgia, in 1982. I have always appreciated that opportunity for service because it allowed me to begin working directly with putting computer technology to work in the local church. First Norcross was the pilot church for Church Information System (CIS) of the Baptist Sunday School Board.

Mike Overcash, at one time the sole employee of CIS, and many others have showed great perseverance over the years. A number of persons were associated with CIS in the early years, while everyone was learning and trying to figure out what was happening. I do not know everyone that was involved, but those with whom I was directly connected included Susan Stevens, Bill Dockrey, Tom Carringer, Clyde Bell, Linda Joines, Butch Savage, Don Davis, and Wanda Wilson.

I must also thank Hugh Garner and the congregation of the First Baptist Church of Waynesville, North Carolina, who not only called me as minister of education in 1985 but also allowed me to recommend that they take the plunge into church computing with CIS. Actually, one forward-thinking church member had already prepared the church to begin planning for a computer before they ever met me. They also gave me the opportunity to work with Sue Smathers who proved that all you have to do to master the computer is not be afraid of it.

I would also like to recognize and thank George Deadwyler and the Bethlehem Baptist Church in Clarkesville, Georgia, for having the faith to call a totally inexperienced young seminary graduate as their first, full-time minister of youth and education.

Finally, I must thank my beautiful wife, Debra, and my two special daughters, Katie and Joy, for support and encouragement and a great deal of love.

1

Computers Are Coming

Would you accept the following offer? As a member of your church, I will make myself available to you twenty-four hours a day. I will keep a full record of every member of your church, every person who is not a church member but is enrolled in some of your organizations such as choir or Sunday School, all prospective members, and anyone else you want to keep up with. Whenever you want a list of names just call me, and I will give it to you in minutes. I can produce the information in almost any printed form you want with practically any range of information about the persons. The names can be sorted any way you want. All you have to do is tell me if you want:
- everyone in Sunday School, arranged by class,
- all single adults who sing in the choir sorted by age,
- youth who are enrolled in Discipleship Training divided into boys and girls and sorted to show whether or not they are church members,
- children ages nine through eleven who have not joined the church.

Would that offer appeal to you? What use could you make of it? Computers offer this capability now. It's not in the future; it is here today. Computers are not unlimited in what they do, but operated properly and with some basic understanding, they really do approach this magnificent offer. If they can do all this, then why should the following situation occur?

A pastor in the South had one basic complaint about the computer system in which his church had invested over $17,000. The system had been in the office for over a year and had produced no results. The system was installed, it was working, the correct programs were present to do the work, and the secretaries had been trained, but nothing was happening. Why? No minister wants to report such a situation to the church. The breakdown had occurred in application. The staff had simply not been able to begin using what was available to them. This scene is being repeated daily all across the country. Some churches will not move forward with a computer because they are afraid they will not know what to do with it.

Is There a Computer in Your Future?

One basic fact facing churches today is that computers are on the way. For example, while no accurate figures are available nationwide, about 17 percent of the churches in the Southern Baptist Convention reported using computers in some manner in 1988. A 1989 survey indicated that 50 percent of Protestant churches owned a computer. Automation and new machines in the office is not a recent development. Churches have gone from manual typewriters, to electric models, and on to sophisticated electronic memory units. They have gone from messy mimeographs, through many types of copiers, to models that copy on plain paper, reduce, enlarge, sort, and collate. Similar advances have been made in adding machines, audiovisual equipment, addressing equipment, and any other type of office automation.

The common factor that has kept automation out of church offices has been price. When machines become affordable, churches begin using them, and that's what is happening with computers today. As computer systems are being more economically priced, churches can afford them, and they are being purchased and installed. In 1982 when the Baptist Sunday School Board introduced its first system for the local church the price tag was about $30,000. Within five years an investment of $10,000 would purchase an equivalent system, but with significantly more speed, memory, and storage capacity. At the time this book was written, a church could purchase a computer system with the capability for word processing and basic records keeping for under $3,500, including computer, printer, and software. While a system for under $3,500 might not be sufficient for many churches, it would enable them to get started. At the same time computers have become readily available; the numbers of church members who use computers in their work has also increased tremendously. The doctor, lawyer, schoolteacher, and auto-parts clerk are all likely to have a computer at work and will use it directly or indirectly. These persons are often the ones who ask, "Doesn't our church need this?"

The Aim Is Application

This book will not dwell on terminology or technology, nor will it dwell on price of systems, configuration of systems, or purchase of systems. This book is designed to be a help in applications for any minister needing information and output. One pastor said, "When the sales representative came to make the presentation to the committee, I felt stupid." He felt that way because he did not understand the technology or the terms being used in the discussion. The sales representative was being asked questions by lay people who were very sophisticated data processing users. The pastor did not understand the terms or the technology. This book takes the approach that the minister does not have to understand what happens inside the box (the computer) or how a computer program is written. A minister does not have to be a builder or know how to read blueprints to be able to use a building. The same comparison holds true for a computer.

If you can dream about what you would do with access to information as described in the opening paragraph, then you can put a computer to use in your church. You will need to understand what your limits are and how to work within the limits of a system. You will also need to understand what kinds of information the computer can give and in what forms the information can be made available. At the beginning of this chapter, the imaginary church member who would give you any information at any time could not read your mind. You still had to ask for what you wanted in a way the person could understand. That is what you must do with the computer. Learn to ask in a way the machine understands. The good news is that learning to ask no longer requires knowledge of computer programming. Good church software has taken care of that.

Churches can obtain computers, but little help is available to tell a minister what can be done with the computer and how the machine can become a tool for ministry. This book focuses on how the computer can be put to maximum use to support the outreach and ministry of the local church. Suggestions are given about what information a minister might request that will help him do the work of ministry. By asking the right questions, you may discover ways that the same facts can be processed to yield different information. This guidance will turn obscure records into a vital, readily accessible, source of information.

What's Special About Computers

While computers are office machines, the computer is inherently different from other office automation. New machines do things better, faster, and sometimes cheaper or with less labor. Computers do this, but they also provide access to people because they give access to information about people. The computer allows direct output of data or information about people. No other office equipment, however sophisticated in design, can make such a claim. The power of a computer with the right programs and the correct data is astonishing. With the use of a computer, the pastor, minister, or staff person has virtually unlimited access to people and information about them. You can begin to approach having that unique helper who will give you whatever information you want.

Churches are people. They exist to bring people together, to train them, and to combine their talents to work to do the work of Christ. Everything about the church is people oriented. **Properly used, the computer finds people instead of losing them.** The computer allows access to people in a way never before possible. Churches often overlook this point as they bring computers into the office. The use of information is a new skill that must be learned. Manual records slow access to information; therefore, church leaders have not generally thought in information terms. Ministers must begin learning to use a new capability.

Laypersons often initiate the process of bringing computers into the church office. In spite of the growing availability of systems, however, in most instances today the minister is not equipped to use the machine because he or she has never had the opportunity to discover what a computer can accomplish. Ministers do not need to become programmers or technicians. They do, however, need to learn to apply the power and functions of computers to enhance and support the ministry and outreach of the church.

The Problems of High Technology

One fact must be admitted: computer technology is confusing and frustrating. When one person talks about computers, the reference is to machines. When another person talks, the reference is to the programs that the machines run. Everyone is afraid of buying something that will become obsolete. As soon as you buy a machine a new one goes on the market. All of this is an inherent problem in the computer industry. Everything electronic is changing. You cannot buy a typewriter, video cassette recorder, or electronic keyboard and not have a new model appear in six to twelve months at the same price with more features. The good news is that with a little study and comparison shopping, you can buy an excellent computer at a reasonable cost that should serve for years.

How does a church make a decision and know it is not making a mistake? How do you protect against obsolescence? One answer is that if you buy something that will do what you bought it to do, as long as it does the job you want, it is not obsolete. The manuscript for this book was typed on a personal computer that is over five years old and by any standard is obsolete. However, it runs reasonably good software and continues to serve well.

The minister trying to help the church make a computer purchasing decision will have to realize that it is a changing industry. Many things that a person might want guaranteed may not be possible. Begin by knowing what you want to do or what you want the computer to accomplish. If you are reading this before buying a computer, then you will have had significant help in knowing what can be done and therefore knowing what you want to do. If you already have a system, this book will help you maximize the use of what you have.

Often when starting to buy a system, a church will make unrealistic demands or have unrealistic expectations. A computer is a machine. A computer does as instructed. It produces what it is capable of producing when asked. If the proper machine is installed with the right printer and the right software, it will do tremendous things. However, it will only do these things if properly used and properly applied. If the software package is very limited the church may become unhappy quickly. To get maximum use from a system, the church may be wiser to start with part of a system that can grow and expand rather than purchase what claims to be a full system at a low cost but actually has severe limitations.

Putting the System to Work

Using the system will always be a tradeoff between making what you do fit what the system does and learning how to make the system do the desired work. With a well-written church software package, you will be able to do what you desire. With a limited package, you will encounter new limitations. There is no system on the market that will "do everything." All systems have some limits. To have one capability you may give up something else. Realizing that the system is not unlimited, and that it must be put to work is the first step toward application.

Church computer use gives its best return on the investment when a computer produces real work and useful information for the church. **Effectively used, computers open infinite new possibilities for ministry and outreach.** The office staff becomes significantly more efficient and responsive. Information is up to date, and reports are available almost instantly. More time is available for more ministry which can be done more effectively.

Computer use is at its worst when the church either buys or is given a system and nothing happens. Letting a system go unused, however, might be better than making partial use of a system. Partial use means entering information incompletely and inaccurately and having no one who knows how to retrieve the information or how to use that information. When information is extracted it is so filled with errors that it cannot be used. In situations like this, one often hears the excuse, "Well we can't get this machine to work."

Good use of a computer system is not difficult, and poor use can certainly be avoided. The only real requirements are time, effort, and a desire to make the system work. Using the system should require little technical knowledge. If a great deal of technical knowledge is required, the wrong system is being used. It is true that computers charge up front in time. The expression *charge up front in time* means that you have to learn to use the system, get the appropriate data in, check and correct the data, and then begin making the applications. The most common reason that is given for why a system or particular program has not been put to use is "we just have not had the time."

The time must be invested. At the start, enough learning has to occur to know how to turn the machine on and begin inputing data, but no one learns everything at the beginning. Learning to use the system becomes an ongoing process. However, you can begin using your system before data is 100 percent entered, and before you know how to do everything with all programs. Information will never be 100 percent complete anyway. The good news is that the time spent in learning to use the computer and inputting data pays great returns in what can be accomplished.

What about Not Getting a Computer?

With all that has been said about the things a computer will do and what a computer can offer, the question remains, is it time for every church to get one? The answer is, every church can put a computer to use, but it may not be time for every church to get one. There are some reasons why a church should not install or invest in a computer.

(1) Don't get a computer for status. The fact that others have one is no reason to purchase a system. Having a poorly used system can be worse than not having a computer. If no one knows why you would want one, other than other churches have them, wait until you find a better reason.

(2) Don't buy one because you love the technology. Churches don't call ministers to have fun with gadgets. If the church has not employed you as a programmer, don't become one. Computer programs are already available to enhance the work of the church. Your time with computers will be best invested in learning to apply these programs to do church work. There is a real temptation to become completely involved in new technology and forget the work the technology should be accomplishing.

(3) Don't buy a computer to solve personnel problems. If people cannot do their work effectively without a computer, there is no particular reason to assume that they will work better with one.

(4) Avoid being "given" a computer, unless it is an IBM (XT, AT, or PS/2) or IBM compatible. Two churches considered letting a local business give them fairly sophisticated mini-computer systems that retailed for over $15,000. When the churches checked further they found that there were very limited possibilities for software and extremely high costs for hardware maintenance. Some churches have been given systems that will do little or nothing but have no option to make a change because all the congregation understands is that the church already has a computer.

By reading this book you will learn how to apply many different types of church management or data base software programs to do the work of the church. Reading and applying the book will not make you a technician, but it should take away the fear of technology and help you approach the computer as a means of furthering the ministry of your church. It is possible for a person to read this book and learn to apply a computer system effectively without ever having to "learn computers."

What Should You Know about
Having a Computer in Your Church?

From what you have read in this chapter you should:

● Know that computers offer significant ways to enhance and support the outreach and ministry of churches.

● Know that this book will focus on how to put computers to use in the church.

2

Try Information Management Not Record Keeping

Every Sunday from many pulpits pastors stress that the church is not the building but the congregation. The church is made up of people, it ministers to people, and it seeks to reach and evangelize new people. Churches meet a need people have to be a part of a group where they feel accepted and loved. It is not uncommon for a church to resist growing because of an uncomfortable feeling that "if we get too large we will not all know one another and the close feeling will be gone." Large churches have often been able to keep the close feeling by having some type of small-group structure within the large organization. Organizations such as Sunday School have filled this roll in many denominations. Small-group structures work well in churches because of the nature of the organization. People need a more intimate nurturing relationship. They will resist changes which seem to threaten the structure that provides such a relationship.

High technology, especially computers, seems to reflect just what churches want to avoid. People don't want to become numbers. Articles that talk about computers in church always include admonitions not to forget that the purpose of the church is to minister. Pastors are reminded that machines can never replace the warmth of the human touch. While technology may seem impersonal, the way to avoid the danger is to use the computer to make ministry more personal. **With computers, church records can become a living, dynamic part of the work of the church.**

Computers may not obviously fit the image of a church, but record keeping has always been a part of church work. Churches keep membership rolls, baptismal records, Sunday School rolls, and many other kinds of records. Church records, particularly baptismal records, can be used in court to establish age. While records are vitally important, record keeping is seldom considered one of the more exciting or dynamic parts of church work and in fact is often woefully neglected.

Record Keeping

Record keeping stresses the correct entry of complete information on the correct form and then having it properly filed. An example would be church membership rolls. When a person comes for membership, he or she would typically fill out some type of application. This would probably include name, address, phone, date of birth, date joining, and the status by which the person becomes a member. When the person is given membership, this information would probably be transferred to whatever constituted the membership roll of the church. Another example would be those who visit the church. If someone visits, his or her name and address need to be made available to the pastor and other appropriate persons and perhaps added to the church's mailing list.

The basic aim of record keeping is to provide complete and accurate information. To keep the data up-to-date requires some degree of guarding and limiting access to the records. The person responsible for the membership roll doesn't want just anyone getting into the cards and perhaps losing or misplacing them. In a typical church system, several files will develop. In the example above, three files were mentioned—the master roll, pastor's personal file, and mailing list. If someone moves, marries, or dies, three files would need to be changed. Most churches will maintain other files, such as stewardship or contribution records, Sunday School or other Christian education rolls, music or choir records, deacon ministry rolls, or mission organization rolls. Once again if records are to be accurate any change must be made in all appropriate places.

Keeping the records is a daunting task. Church records require more than just name, address, and phone number. Dates such as when a person comes for membership or is baptized, born, or married, must also be kept. Exactly what dates are significant will depend on the individual church.

If a membership roll is kept accurately and up-to-date, it is probably done by one person who has a commitment to that specific task. It is a practical impossibility to make creative use of the information, not because of the person keeping the records, but because it is a manual system. Simple information like the names of family members who have not joined the church is probably not kept. A list of single adults in the church might be needed but would require a major effort to obtain. Any church that has done a pictorial directory knows the effort required to make a list of names, addresses, and phone numbers for the directory.

The following points sum up the typical system of manual record keeping:

(1) The best that can be hoped for is accuracy and completeness.

(2) Access to the records is limited.

(3) Multiple files will exist and will become inaccurate as changes occur and are not made in all files.

(4) Retrieving simple selected or special lists becomes tedious and very time consuming.

(5) Keeping simple information not directly related to the record is not done. For example on a church membership record, the names of family members not in the church may not be kept nor would marital status normally be recorded although both are important.

It is not surprising that churches have trouble keeping up with their members. Keeping up with potential or prospective members increases the difficulties. Because prospective members are in fact prospective, information is almost certain to be incomplete. The point of keeping information on prospective members is to make use of it in some way to contact the persons. Prospective member records in most churches often consist of cards the visitors filled out when they attended the church. Kept somewhere in the church office, the cards are seldom used because the information (what is on the cards) cannot be effectively made available.

If careful thought is given to this situation it will be seen that the information called "records" represents the church's or the minister's ability to keep up with people. People are the church and if the church cannot correctly maintain at least the address, phone number, and membership status then the people are lost to the church and often forgotten. Record keeping that is done well can insure that somewhere in a file accurate, although limited, information can be found. That is not enough, and it is not what a minister must settle for any longer.

Information Management

Few persons think in information management terms, yet today, in any size church, a minister manages information. In fact, a small church may be able to have better information management than the largest churches. Information management goes beyond record keeping to the ability to access church records as usable information. Putting information to work makes the difference between record keeping and information management.

Computers are different from other office machines because they have the power to process data and output information in an endless number of ways. When this power is applied to church records, the minister finds information available literally at one's fingertips. Such a claim does have restrictions. Availability of data depends on (1) the speed and capacity of the machine, (2) the capability of the software, and (3) the extent and quality of data entered, but even with restrictions the possibilities are tremendous. A task that once took days may now be completed in minutes.

An example will make this capability more clear. Assume that for a group of 500 individuals the following information is recorded on 4- by 6-inch cards and filed in a box: name, address, phone number, and date of birth. How long would it take to get a list of all men, ages twenty-one and up, a list of these men with their phone numbers, and a set of mailing labels? The information is available in the sense that it exists, but it is practically unavailable because of the time required to do the task. If the same information were placed on a computer with an indication of whether the person was male or female, the information could be ready in five or ten minutes in both forms (a list and mailing labels) using most types of church software. Furthermore, the more detail each record has, the more types of information that are available. **Information management not only keeps files and records but extracts useful information in useful forms to support and enhance the work of the church.**

There are practical considerations for specific situations. A file containing 4000 records with extensive information on each person will require a more powerful computer than a file containing only 400 records. Such considerations must be addressed in purchasing a system, but an important matter at this point is to consider the possibilities of having information available.

The potential for managing information with a computer goes beyond the types of information that can be selected. A computer system offers a variety of kinds of *output.* Output in this case is what actually comes out of the machine in printed form. What is needed? Is it a list of names, names and addresses, 3- by 5-inch cards, a church directory, or perhaps mailing labels? Many other types of output are possible.

When output is considered, we return to the comparison of a manual versus a computer record-keeping system. With a manual record-keeping system, record cards would never be allowed to leave the church office after they were filed. To take information from the records would involve tediously copying it into the desired form. With the computer, regardless of how much information is output or how many forms the data takes, the records remain securely in the storage device inside the computer. The information can be put into numerous printed formats with equal ease.

Putting a Computer to Use

A point needs to be introduced that can make the difference between whether a computer decision is a total waste of money or a significant step forward in the work of the church. **A computer is made for information processing. It is a waste to use a computer as a glorified typewriter or electronic file cabinet.** The difference between simply being an electronic file cabinet and an information processing system is whether the output is in a form that produces usable information. Computers should be producing needed and usable information. This implies that someone is asking for information and using information. This brings us back to the imaginary church member in chapter 1. Having a person who could produce at will any type of information would be worthless unless someone used the capability. Having a machine that could do the same function would be of no benefit to the church unless the machine was used. Church leaders must take the initiative in the use of the information.

Using the information requires some understanding of both the capabilities and limitations of the system, but this understanding does not have to be technical. If the minister takes a hands off, "it makes me nervous, I don't want to know" attitude then it is almost guaranteed that the system will never be fully used. Effective use only comes when the system becomes a tool for information processing to minister to and reach people. Ministers must lead in using information for outreach and ministry.

Information management makes the computer a personalizing rather than a de-personalizing office tool. **The quickest way to lose people is to put their name and address on cards and file them.** That name may never been seen again. If a person or family moves, the address might be updated or might not. Church rolls are full of such forgotten persons. Information processing can help solve this problem. The forgotten person's name often appears on lists. Whether the list is all members, women, singles, senior adults, or all four, the name keeps coming back. Having the access to the information about people makes it much more likely that a committed minister can keep up with the congregation in an effective manner. Putting a computer to use is a leadership/staff responsibility.

Another consideration affects information processing—incomplete and missing data. No church will ever have a list of all the birthdays or wedding anniversaries. They may even have some Lynn's, Shane's, or other names and not know whether the individual is male or female. Addresses and phone numbers likewise will probably always have minor errors. Information processing assumes the user is aware of this fact of life. Whatever is done in the way of mailing labels or reports should always be checked. The machine is limited to the data in it, and the data will never be 100 percent complete or correct.

Software to Do the Work

A computer is an electronic device that can store, process, and print data. The machine does not know or care what type of data is being worked on. The data might be complex mathematical formulas, weather information, interest rates, words, tax returns, or it might be the names and addresses of your church members. The computer needs instructions to tell the machine to work on church member information rather than football statistics. Those instructions are called *programs* or *software.*

When a church considers buying a computer, a typical question is: What kind of computer do we need? This is the wrong question. The first question should be: What do we want to do? Answering this question will point the church to the kind of software needed and the software will point the church to the computer system needed.

An analogy might be helpful. Ministers know that if they are going to lead a church to build a building the first question is what do we want to do or what do we need? Is the building to be used for recreation, worship, education, or some combination of all three? Answers to these questions will determine what type of building will be built.

Many different types of software are available and applicable to a church office. If you have read about church software or if you have a computer with software, you may already know that there are two basic approaches to keeping church records on the computer.

The first approach is to use some type of general data base software package and design your own record-keeping system. A *data base program*, as the name implies, works from a base of data or information. It allows the user to create a system for keeping records. There are a number of programs that can be purchased in retail stores to maintain records. These programs could be used in a doctor's office, lawyer's office, real estate office, or in a church. The operator specifies what information will be kept and how it is to be kept. The program provides various means of entering data, selecting data entered, and printing reports. A sophisticated data base will allow the operator to do almost anything, but the operator must be able to define exactly what is to be done.

The other approach is to purchase a church record-keeping system designed specifically for churches. Either approach can do the work of information processing. Either approach can significantly enhance the capabilities of the church. You should decide which approach is best for your church.

Using Standard Data Bases

The general argument for taking a standard data base and designing your own software is that it is cheaper, and a person can do anything with a data base that can be done with church management software. While with a sophisticated data base this may be technically true, practically, it is incorrect. It is true that good data base packages can be purchased for under $300 and that church management software costs from $400 to several thousand dollars depending on the vendor and how much software is purchased. Cost aside, the advantages begin to swing quickly in the direction of buying software designed for the church application. If you are thinking of setting up your own data base system, you should consider five important points.

(1) Designing a data base requires a great deal of understanding of computer technology, logic, and programming that the typical minister does not have, does not want, and does not need. What is saved in money will be lost in someone's time. Setting up a data base is time consuming. This process gets you to the point of being ready to enter member information. You will have to decide what information will be kept, how the screen will be laid out, how the data base can perform functions like categorizing persons both as individuals and as members of a family, and how it can calculate ages from birth dates. One pastor had a member who insisted that he could setup a data base to do what the software they wanted to purchase could do. The pastor agreed to let the member try and gave him six months. Six months later the originally planned purchase was made.

(2) Setting up a data base usually will focus on a single application. For example the data base might produce mailing labels or a directory. Later, when the staff decides it needs to print Sunday School class rolls, the data base must be enhanced or modified. A data base can easily handle names

and addresses for a mailing list, but once this application is in process new needs are discovered. Keeping birth dates, sex, and marital status requires another enhancement. Subsequent improvements in the data base depend on the programmer having time available. The person who did the design must be available to keep the system enhanced and running.

(3) Integrated data bases are difficult to design. A data base may be created to keep names, addresses, phone numbers, birth dates, and marital status. To go beyond that and allow keeping stewardship contributions, attendance information, and prospect information is far from simple. In a well-designed church management system the person's name and address data is entered once, and the additional data may be kept for other functions without having to re-enter the basic name and address information.

(4) The data base must be created before others can be trained. How the system operates will be clear to the designer but it must be something that can be transferred to another person. A church in the Midwest had a data base set up to keep contribution records. The member who created the program moved. No one knew how to operate the system, so the church purchased a stewardship package that worked with the membership software they already had.

(5) Well-designed church software makes technical computer knowledge almost unnecessary. Easy-to-read menus, fill-in-the-blank screens, and readily available help messages allow the user to operate the computer system without knowing much about the computer itself.

Having pointed out some of the pitfalls of designing your own system, it must be said that there is a place for using a data base. A minister who already possesses necessary knowledge and perhaps has his or her own computer and data base software can make effective use of a simple, data base design.

Typically, a church will set up a computer system because it is an aid to ongoing work, outreach, and ministry. Therefore, **it seems unwise to invest money in machines and then fail to buy the software that will enable the machines to do all they are capable of doing.** Well-designed, well-documented, and well-supported church software is the best answer for most churches. The final chapters in the book will return to a discussion of system purchasing and hardware considerations and will include a discussion of multi-user versus single-user systems, printers, and some guidelines to follow in purchasing both hardware and software. Some suggestions for evaluating software will also be given.

What Should You Know about
Information Management?

From what you have read in this chapter you should:

• Know that computers offer you the ability to manage information.

• Understand that information management is the ability to put information to use by putting it into a usable form.

3

Keeping Up with People

An Arkansas mission church called to ask about obtaining church software. Mission churches seldom have a great deal of money to invest in office equipment, but the woman keeping the church records was interested in the possibility of computer software. She wanted to know if it was appropriate for a new church to start off with a computer. The answer is *yes*. It would be a great thing to do. If a new church began using a computer system, then 100 years later they could potentially recall the name of any person who had been a member and know when and how that person joined, the date and reason he or she left. To do this, a church would need effective software, properly maintained and used over the time indicated.

At least thirty different companies sell church management software. In addition there are an infinite number of approaches to data base designs for church software. Regardless of the number of possible software packages, the same type of information is being kept for generally the same purposes in all situations. **The fact that churches maintain similar information for similar purposes makes this book possible.** While examples of information use will probably not be exactly what your church does, the examples should suggest many possible approaches that will help you accomplish the work you need to do.

No attempt will be made to tell you how to operate a specific software package. The vendor should provide help with operation, documentation, training, and support. Your software may not do all of the things suggested in this and following chapters. All applications described can be done with church software produced by Church Information System of the Baptist Sunday School Board in Nashville, Tennessee. The aim of this chapter is to get you started using what you have to support and enhance ministry. This is true whether you are just starting or have had a system for some time.

You Must Get in and Get Started

The minister starting to experiment with a system for the first time must be willing to experience some frustration. This frustration involves finding out how to move about in the software, look things up, and select or print information. If a little time is devoted to learning, the user should come fairly quickly to a point of seeing what can be done and how the software can be used.

If you are a minister who has decided to find out what an existing system will do, you should be prepared to hear comments like "our system will not do that." This will especially be true if the system has not been used to great extent. A bright woman was hired to be the Sunday School records secretary for a large church in Alabama. She had no fears about using the computer system the church had. She simply went to work and began trying things. When she would call the person she replaced to ask questions, the new person would often hear the former worker exclaim, "I didn't know we could do that!" Persons who operate a system may only find out how to do the minimum to get the prescribed job done and not seek out the full capabilities of the system. It is often easier to say, "Our system will not do that," or "That would take too much time," than it is to take the time to learn how to do what is desired.

While there may be some applications a system might not do, there should be few if any applications that good systems will not at least offer help in doing. Getting the maximum use requires working with the system, reading the manuals, asking questions, being willing to make mistakes, and trying again. If the system proves truly limited and if the vendor cannot provide assistance that would be a signal to consider different software.

Start with Basic Information

Most applications involve basic member information. If basic information is not kept accurately and cannot be accessed easily then all other applications will break down. If the minister will first learn to use and manage basic information then he or she will move much more quickly to more sophisticated uses for the system. **Systems are not used for two primary reasons—lack of interest on the part of the staff and trying to do advanced applications without getting basic information entered and basic use of the system mastered.**

The first question then would be: What is basic information? Every church should want to have the following items on each member: name, address, phone number, date of birth, date joined church, how joined church, sex, and marital status. Additionally, this information should be entered in such a way that families are seen as units. The church should know the basic information for spouses and children who are in the family but not yet members of the church.

Membership software works on the basis of having one large file in which everyone for whom the church keeps a name and address is entered. All names and addresses go in the file and various codes or flags are used to indicate member status. You need to picture in your mind this concept of one large file for all persons as you begin using membership software. Everyone, regardless of status, goes into the same file. It would be like taking a thousand 3- by 5-inch cards with names, addresses, and phone numbers and putting them in a hopper, but having the ability to pull out all of the cards for church members or all cards for prospective church members. Effective use of a code to indicate membership status is the first step in information management using the computer. We will call this code *church relationship*. Possible church relationship codes might include:

Code	Meaning	Definition
A	Resident Church Member	A church member who lives in the local church community or area.
P	Prospective Church Member	Someone the church considers a prospective church member. The code could apply to family members who are not yet members of the church.
F	Friend of the Church	Could be used for a spouse who is an active member of another church, a former member who has moved but still maintains a relationship with the church, or anyone who does not fit another category.
N	Non-Resident Church Member	A church member who has never been removed from the

		roll but has moved away. The address may or may not be known.
S	Sunday School Member Only	Would designate a person enrolled in Sunday School or Christian education who has not yet joined the church. Many children might fit this category.

For churches that actively use the Sunday School, it may prove useful to break the resident church member code into two separate codes, such as resident church member enrolled in Sunday School and resident church member not enrolled in Sunday School.

Many more codes could be devised. However, the codes should be limited to what is required to indicate basic membership status. While having a code to indicate inactive members may seem desirable, careful thought should be given before using such a code. The problem with an inactive code is defining what an inactive member is and being able to keep the code accurate. If inactive is defined based on attendance, giving, or receiving communion, and if that information can be correctly obtained and regularly checked and updated then an inactive code would have meaning. If however, the term inactive is a subjective judgment (based on whether the person has been seen lately) on the part of a minister, clerk, or secretary and is never updated then the use of the code could corrupt the system before it could be used. Membership status should be clear-cut, uniform, easily verified, and easily updated based on known, obtainable information.

If this basic information described above were available to you, what could be done with it? Only eight items of information have been suggested. In computer terms each of the eight items is called a *field*. The eight fields of information for each person comprise a record. All of the records together make up the "membership file."[1] Using the analogy of the 3- by 5-inch cards in a hopper, the name on a card would be a *field*, the card would be a *record*, and the hopper containing all the cards would be a *file*. Assume you can search the membership file based on the fields. You might produce any of following lists of names:

- Resident church members
- Single adult church members

- Youth ages 12-17
- Women ages 25-45 who are either church members, Sunday School members, or both.
- Adults over 62
- Preschoolers living in a specific zip code
- Babies born within the last six months
- Members with birth dates in June
- Adults who were baptized in the last five years.

These options should be sufficient to indicate the power and capability available when information can be accessed in various ways. The challenge is to make use of what can be done. Church software keeps more than eight fields. It must be stressed however that while more can be kept, the utility of the system comes in keeping the most basic information as complete as possible, up-to-date, and accurate. Most of the information selected will come from basic data.

Going Beyond Basic Information

What additional information might be kept? Other fields could include title (Mr., Mrs., Dr., and so forth), Christian education or other organizational enrollment, business information, extra date fields, notes on persons, multiple addresses, visit area,[2] and special profiles.[3] The profile code area is mentioned frequently in advertising. The ability to keep information on talents, interests, blood type, and other similar data normally comes through profile codes. It must be emphasized that a church would be wise to master keeping the basic data and putting it to use before trying to do more sophisticated applications. There are several reasons for this.

(1) If the basic name, address, and phone data is not right, then the entire file will be of little use.

(2) If the church relation data is not entered and correct, few meaningful selections can be made.

(3) Most of the actual work and usable reports will still come from basic data even when the more unique information is entered.

Whether or not a piece of information should be kept on the system is an important question. Most systems allow the church to keep more information than the minister can practically use or the secretary can effectively maintain. Some questions that would help you make a decision on keeping a piece or type of data would include.

(1) Is the data needed?

(2) Who needs it and why?

(3) If you had the data who would use it?

(4) Do you have a known means of getting the data?

(5) Do you have a known means of updating the data?

(6) Do you know who would be responsible for gathering, entering, and updating the data?

The choice of basic information will vary from church to church. In churches that emphasize Sunday School, information on Sunday School enrollment is basic. In a denomination that emphasizes communion dates, the date communion was last taken would be important. Any selection must be made knowing that some data could be missing from a record and therefore would cause that record to not be selected.

Once you have a clear idea of the potential for selecting lists of names based on the information being kept, the next step is to add the ability to sort in different ways. Consider a list of church members. The same list of church members would produce entirely different results depending on whether it was sorted alphabetically by name, alphabetically by family, by zip code, by age from oldest to youngest, or by date the member joined from the oldest to newest member. Church software should provide extensive capabilities for sorting, and multiple-level sorts should be possible.

The possibilities created by *multi-level sorts* are used to point out what computers can do with data. For example, a minister might decide to sort the church membership first by how the person joined and then by age. Think about what sorting in this manner might tell you. You could see at a glance the age spread of persons who had joined by baptism and the age spread of persons who had joined by transfer from other churches.

Two steps in retrieving useful information from a computer—deciding what criteria define the list of persons needed and determining how the information should be sorted—have already been given. A third step is to produce an output of the information. The most common output is some type of printed report.[4] Examples would include mailing labels for the youth, a directory of choir members, or 3- by 5-inch cards of new members for the pastor to use in calling.

With the information you have on (1) keeping information, (2) selecting lists based on information kept, (3) sorting the lists, and (4) choosing an appropriate output, you should be able to begin deciding how to use a computer system for information management in significant ways. If you do not yet have a system, you should be able to evaluate the capabilities of various software packages to see if they provide the functions you will require.

Making Applications

Examples of information processing using membership software will clarify how the software is used and suggest applications you should consider. Assume you are in an older church in a stable community. A concern you often hear voiced is that there are not as many young adults with families in the church as there used to be. How could you use the computer to tell you just what the situation is? There are several questions that might need to be answered. One would be: What is the actual distribution of ages in the current church membership? Another question might be: What is the age distribution of persons joining our church?

The age distribution of the membership should be simple to obtain. Use the selection capability of the software to obtain a count of church members in the age ranges desired. You might specify: under 7, 7-11, 12-17, 18-21, 22-29, 30-39, 40-49, 50-59, 60-69, 70-79, 80-89, and 90 up. Probably each age range would have to be a separate selection. The church relationship code, or whatever code indicates member status, would be a part of the selection since the information desired is based on counting those who are members and excluding persons in the file who are not members. For this part of the process only numbers would be needed. You could create a selection statement that might read:

> Church Relation $=$ Resident Member
> and   Age $>$ 12
> and   Age $<$ 17

This particular selection would list all persons over age 12 and under age 17 who are resident church members.

Doing the selection by ages would not be completely accurate since all persons might not have their birthdays listed. If a significant number of birthdays were missing the data could be very inaccurate. Some software packages have the capability to select based on the field in question being blank. However, even without this possibility, you should be able to select all persons in the desired member status and sort the selection by age. All persons with no birth dates would be grouped either at the end or the beginning of the printout and could be easily counted. It should be possible to estimate the age ranges of the persons whose birthdays are not listed. Other information, such as Sunday School class, might give an estimate of age. Counting the members in the age ranges set up by the operator and combining it with the information on estimated ages should easily and quickly produce the age distribution of the membership.

The second directly related question would be: What is the distribution of ages of persons joining the church? The selection procedure should be used to create a list of all persons who joined the church in the last year. This might be done by selecting based on date joined or on how many months they have been members. The list could be sorted by age and printed with name, age, and date joined. Figure 1 shows a printout of actual church data[5] for members who joined within the past twelve months.

Sorting by age would immediately show the needed breakdown. Looking at Figure 1 it seems that this church is receiving adults 50 and below. Some ages are missing but the age distribution of new members is apparent. The time period might be one month, twelve months, two years, or five years. It might be interesting to do several selections using persons who joined in the last year (0 to 12 months), persons who joined five years ago (48 to 60 months), or persons who joined ten years ago (108 to 120 months). Comparing lists might indicate whether the percentage of persons coming into the church from various age groups had changed over time. For the same church, Figure 2 shows the same selection for persons who have been members from 108 to 120 months or who joined from nine to ten years ago.

A minister comparing the information in Figure 2 to the information in Figure 1 would have to remember that the persons in Figure 2 were ten years younger when they joined. Obviously most of the birth dates are missing in the second list. However knowing some ages and probably knowing many of the persons by name on the list would still make it possible to estimate the age distribution of the persons who joined ten years ago. It appears that this church is receiving new members from a young and median adult group. This example shows how information can be selected for membership analysis, and it is also likely that as a minister studied the lists of names, ministry needs would also come to mind. Remember the statement in chapter 2 that as lists are selected, names appear regardless of whether they are attending regularly or not. This provides a constant reminder about people.

Figure 1.

BSME0405 1.05
04/09/89
5 Members 0-12 Month

Any Church
ABBREVIATED MEMBERSHIP MASTER LIST
04/09/89

FAMILY ID	NAME	ADDRESS		PHONE	CHURCH RELATION	JOIN DATE	AGE
7100-12	Reilly, Charles	103 Elm Street	City, ST 45321		A	9/11/88	8
31900-12	House, Karen	408 Old Oak Drive	City, ST 45321	724-1336	A	2/05/89	9
36000-12	Tucker, Jamie	20 Sand Creek Lane	City, ST 45321	724-6130	A	9/25/88	10
2350-13	Baker, Sam	176 Morning Road	City, ST 45321	653-5291	A	9/11/88	12
36000-11	Tucker, Amy	20 Sand Creek Lane	City, ST 45321	724-6130	A	9/25/88	16
7200-11	Wright, Mitch	Rt 6, Box 231	City, ST 45321		A	9/18/88	16
23050-11	Morgan, Wesley	211 Wallstone Drive	City, ST 45321	653-0672	A	7/31/88	17
2300-12	Ducket, Wanda	310 Woodstone Circle	City, ST 45321	653-6222	A	5/01/88	18
21990-01	Lawrence, Donald	351 South Main	City, ST 45321	724-6571	B	9/25/88	19
23040-02	Morgan, Tammy	101 Martha Street	City, ST 45321	653-6423	B	10/23/88	25
39700-02	Whitson, Tom	67 Village Lane	City, ST 45321	724-4081	A	4/17/88	27
225-02	Adams, Linda	134 Franklin Pike	City, ST 45321	724-1014	B	9/04/88	28
36200-01	James, Mark	107 Oakland	City, ST 45321	724-1384	A	8/07/88	28
7100-02	Richards, Doris	12 High Street Drive	City, ST 45321		A	8/31/88	31
36200-02	James, Margaret	107 Oakland	City, ST 45321	724-1384	A	8/07/88	31
72480-02	Thomas, Benny	402 Clearview Drive	City, ST 45321	724-0379	A	9/14/88	32
31900-02	House, Mary	408 Old Oak Drive	City, ST 45321	724-1336	A	2/05/89	33
36000-01	Tucker, Bill	20 Sand Creek Lane	City, ST 45321	724-6130	A	9/25/88	40
36000-02	Tucker, Cheryl	20 Sand Creek Lane	City, ST 45321	724-6130	A	9/25/88	41
6250-02	Davis, Linda	124 Chase Trail	City, ST 45321	653-3199	B	1/15/89	43
33900-01	Smith, Joe	134 South Hall Rd	City, ST 45321	653-7311	A	2/26/89	50
33900-02	Smith, Lou	134 South Hall Rd	City, ST 45321	653-7311	A	2/26/89	52
22000-01	Lawrence, Keith	51 South First	City, ST 45321	724-6571	A	8/28/88	
22000-02	Lawrence, Lana	51 South First	City, ST 45321	724-6571	A	8/28/88	
22000-11	Lawrence, Betty	51 South First	City, ST 45321	724-6571	A	8/28/88	
33400-02	Black, Peggy	873 Old Mill Road	City, ST 45321	653-0014	B	2/19/89	
33400-11	Black, Mandy	873 Old Mill Road	City, ST 45321	653-0014	B	5/22/88	

Figure 2.

BSME0405 1.06
04/09/89
7 Members 108-120 Mont

Any Church
ABBREVIATED MEMBERSHIP MASTER LIST
04/09/89

PAGE: 1
CHURCH RELATIONSHIP CODES:

FAMILY ID	NAME	ADDRESS			PHONE	CHURCH RELATION	JOIN DATE	AGE
25000-02	Morris, Tom	Rt 4, Walnut Lane	City, ST	45321	321-1484	B	12/16/79	17
23020-01	Morgan, Luke	100 Polk Place	City, ST	45321	321-5710	B	4/20/80	19
23020-02	Morgan, Sheila	100 Polk Place	City, ST	45321	321-5710	B	5/04/80	20
4300-12	Ronson, Bruce	713 Waynewood Drive	City, ST	45321	321-2572	A	2/02/80	21
26000-02	Oakley, Pam	706 Bell Drive	City, ST	45321	321-6516	B	12/01/79	24
39400-11	Webb, Tommy	516 College Street	City, ST	45321	321-0402	A	4/29/79	25
40000-02	Wilson, Susan	119 East Spring	City, ST	45321		B	7/29/79	33
22400-02	McCann, James	PO Box 254	City, ST	45321	321-1977	B	4/29/79	45
34050-01	Stevens, Mark	536 W. Main	City, ST	45321		B	11/18/79	46
33500-02	Schultz, Sara	102 Gillis Street	City, ST	45321	321-0995	B	7/01/79	47
20000-01	Lang, Alton	303 Davis Park Drive	City, ST	45321	321-6652	B	11/04/79	54
2300-01	Ball, John	310 Wildwood Circle	City, ST	45321	321-6222	A	4/29/79	
4300-01	Ronson, Jerry	713 Waynewood Drive	City, ST	45321	321-2572	A	2/02/80	
4300-02	Ronson, Terri	713 Waynewood Drive	City, ST	45321	321-2572	A	2/02/80	
4300-11	Ronson, Joe	713 Waynewood Drive	City, ST	45321	321-2572	A	2/02/80	
4480-02	Cox, Barbara	3211 Elm Street	City, ST	45321		B	5/13/79	
5500-02	Currey, Lynn	Lee's Park	City, ST	45321	321-9566	B	1/14/80	
12080-01	Gentry, Jason					A	12/02/79	
12100-02	Hill, Darby	PO Box 376	City, ST	45321	321-7661	A	5/13/79	
13500-02	James, Christy	Rt 9	City, ST	45321	321-8180	B	7/29/79	
14100-12	Hale, Jimmy	113 Church Street	City, ST	45321		B	8/05/79	
14300-01	Harris, Dale	PO Box 8809	City, ST	45321		B	5/15/79	
14400-01	Herndon, Charles	Rt 1	City, ST	45321	321-6811	B	5/13/79	
14600-01	Hinley, Mike	Mitchell Lane	City, ST	45321	321-2891	B	6/03/79	
14600-02	Hinley, Caron	Mitchell Lane	City, ST	45321	321-3779	B	6/03/79	
20000-02	Lawrence, Bill	703 Park Drive	City, ST	45321	321-6652	B	11/04/79	
20000-01	Lawrence, Randy	703 Park Drive	City, ST	45321	321-6652	B	11/04/79	
20000-12	Lawrence, Patsy	703 Park Drive	City, ST	45321	321-6652	B	11/04/79	
22100-01	Martin, Clarence	PO Box 534	City, ST	45321	321-2718	B	12/09/79	
22100-02	Martin, Sara	PO Box 534	City, ST	45321	321-2718	B	12/02/79	
22320-02	Maxey, James	14 Main Street	City, ST	45321	321-5043	B	8/05/79	
22350-01	Jones, Eddie	Box 31	City, ST	45321		B	2/17/80	
22800-01	Miller, Jack	321 William Drive	City, ST	45321	321-3048	B	6/22/79	
22800-02	Miller, Peggy	321 William Drive	City, ST	45321	321-3048	B	6/22/79	
23200-01	Norris, Rich	2019 East Lane	City, ST	45321	321-2148	B	1/20/80	
23200-02	Norris, Lana	2019 East Lane	City, ST	45321	321-2148	B	1/20/80	
23200-11	Norris, Joy	2019 East Lane	City, ST	45321	321-2148	B	1/20/80	
23500-01	Murphy, Pete	1107 Davis Blvd	City, ST	45321	321-6487	B	11/11/79	

Checking the Data

As you think about doing selections as described in the example, the need for accurate information becomes apparent. Regular checking of data should be done to insure accuracy. Records could be checked by looking at each member record on screen. However, to check fifteen or twenty fields on each record as you move through several hundred records would probably not be effective. Different types of printouts should be done to check specific types of data. This would be a worthwhile effort for ministers. It has been estimated that 95 percent of the churches in the United States have fewer than 1000 members. If the membership of a 1000-member church were printed in a one line per member format with fifty names per page this would require twenty pages. Scanning twenty pages is not an unreasonable or overly time consuming task.

What might you discover if you asked for a complete membership printout, alphabetically by family unit, listing name, address, phone number, birth date, church relationship code, and Christian education (or Sunday School) enrollment? Thirty minutes spent in scanning such a report could tell you:

(1) Members whose addresses and phone numbers are not listed.

(2) Members whose birth dates are not known.

(3) Members who have not been assigned church relationship codes.

(4) Members not enrolled in Christian education.

(5) Cases where one family member is listed at a different address from other members, which could indicate an incorrect address.

(6) Typing or data entry errors in names, addresses, or phone numbers.

Study Figure 3 and see how easy it is to spot these items. Examining printouts often suggests new uses for information, and the computer system increasingly works for you.

Many systems use some form of assigned member number to access records quickly and also to keep family units together. If the number is assigned by the operator it would appear on the printout as noted in Figure 3. In systems that use numbers, the number is usually the quickest way to access or retrieve a member record to make corrections. Software packages that do not use numbers should provide some means of quickly finding an individual record. Regardless of whether numbers are used or not, a staff member could mark corrections on a printout and give the

Figure 3.

BSME0405 1.06
04/09/89
8 All Members

Any Church
ABBREVIATED MEMBERSHIP MASTER LIST
04/09/89

PAGE:

FAMILY ID	NAME	ADDRESS			PHONE	CHURCH RELATION	ENROLLED DEPT/CLS	BIRTH DATE
12000-01	Banion, Joe	197 Springs Rd	City, ST	45321	321-1451	A	A/Sen	4/20/21
12000-02	Banion, Sue	197 Springs Rd	City, ST	45321	321-1451	A	C/C5	11/01/23
12050-01	Bowman, Jack	6 South Oak Dr	City, ST	45321	321-3916	B		7/19/27
12050-02	Bowman, Ron	6 South Oak Drive	City, ST	45321	321-3916	B		6/13/40
12060-02	Bowman, Jackie					B		12/06/69
12070-01	Bowman, Jerry					B		9/06/70
12080-01	Bowman, Jason					B		
12100-02	Cline, Randi	31 North Pike	City, ST	45321	321-7661	A	A/CAD	
12100-11	Cline, John	425 Eagle Lake Lane	City, ST	45321	321-7661	A	Y/G7	6/22/74
12100-12	Cline, Rich	31 North Pike	City, ST	45321	321-7661	A	C/C3	10/15/78
12500-01	Cole, Joe, Jr.	812 Eastview Drive	City, ST	45321	321-9290	A	A/Men	7/22/42
12500-02	Cole, Wanda	812 Eastview Drive	City, ST	45321	321-9290	A	A/CAD	8/09/44
12500-11	Cole, Joe, Jr.	812 East Drive	City, ST	45321	321-9290	A	A/CC	9/18/70
12500-12	Cole, Ronald	812 Eastview Drive	City, ST	45321	321-9290	A	Y/B9	8/13/72
12800-01	Collins, Thomas	985 Oakland Heights	City, ST	45321	321-4216	B		
12800-02	Collins, Linda	321 Oakland Heights	City, ST	45321	321-4216	B		
12900-01	Deaver, Pearl	456 Stewarts Lane	City, ST	45321	321-6724	A	A/Sen	3/25/28
12900-02	Deaver, Lonny	456 Stewarts Lane	City, ST	45321	321-6724	A		
13000-01	Dendy, David	456 Stewarts Lane	City, ST	45321		B		5/14/58
13500-02	Deills, Charles	Rt 9	City, ST	45321	321-8180	B		
14100-01	Edwards, John	233 Church Street	City, ST	45321		B		
14200-01	Estes, William	415 Woodbury Drive	City, ST	45321	321-4322	B		4/08/32
14200-02	Estes, Carolyn	415 Woodbury Drive	City, ST	45321	321-4322	B		
14200-11	Evans, Derry	415 Woodbury Drive	City, ST	45321	321-4322			
14200-12	Evans, Kim	415 Woodbury Drive	City, ST	45321	321-4322			7/02/64
14300-01	Farmer, Dale	988 Jackson Road			321-6811	B		
14400-01	Faulkner, Arles	Box 241	City, ST	45321	321-2891	B		
14500-02	Fisher, Sandra	349 Mitchell Blvd			321-2639	B		4/28/45
14600-01	Ford, Mike	891 Mitchell Blvd	City, ST	45321	321-3779	B		
14600-02	Ford, Carol	891 Mitchell Blvd	City, ST	45321	321-3779			
14900-02	Forrister, Lawrence	200 Carry Street	City, ST	45321	321-4081	B		9/23/61

printout to a secretary or church clerk so corrections could be made on the system. A practical suggestion is to throw away such printouts once they have been used for their intended purpose. If your church generates a large amount of printouts, you may want to explore the possibility of recycling. You need to think of the computer file being the official or correct church roll. Any printout is a one time check of the information shown. The printout was only up-to-date when it was done. Once corrections have been made, the printout should be discarded.

At this point you should have an understanding of the various aspects of church membership software. **The two key requirements for effective use of such software are: (1) a commitment to putting the system to work to support the outreach and ministry of the church, and (2) imagination.** No matter how much training is taken or how much documentation is read, there is no way to learn or understand any software package without sitting at a keyboard, trying to do things, making mistakes, and trying again. With a general understanding of keeping basic records it is possible to move to other church software applications.

What Should You Know about Keeping up with People?

From what you have read in this chapter you should:

• Know that keeping effective membership records on the computer starts with well-maintained, basic information.

• Understand that membership applications require thought and direction from pastor and staff.

Notes

1. This definition of files is generally true but may not be specifically or technically true for all software packages.

2. *Visit area* is a code entered to indicate the geographic area in which a person lives.

3. Some vendors use the term *profile* to mean any details kept on an individual. In this book the term refers to special information the operator decides to keep beyond basic data.

4. Other outputs include viewing on screen or creating a disk file but these operations are not critical to understanding how to use membership software.

5. Whenever data is printed, names and addresses have been changed; however, birth dates, dates joined, and the presence or absence of data in specific fields is correct for an actual church.

4

Keeping Up with What Is Given

Maintaining stewardship or contribution records is a perfect application for a computer. Churches keep contribution records primarily to furnish their members a statement of giving for their tax records. While some churches still do not maintain records of contribution, it can be safely said that most churches do. In many churches these are the most confidential records kept. Some churches make it a policy to hire a secretary who is not a member of the church so that no church member will know what anyone gives. Other churches will print in the church newsletter the giving of each member for each week.

Entering Contributions

Regardless of whether the giving records are completely secret or public knowledge, the computer provides an ideal means of maintaining and storing the information. A church can generally save secretarial hours by installing a computer; however, this will not always be the case. Adding a computer to the office will probably facilitate enough new ways of doing things to keep the current secretarial force employed. However, the area in which the computer saves the most time and labor is keeping stewardship records. Basic stewardship record keeping is simple. The operator enters the person, the fund the money was given to, and the amount. Often the giving is entered by a number assigned to the person.

Using a number is not new. Many churches who do not use computers already give their members numbered offering envelopes. This envelope number can usually be assigned as the number used for entering contribution records in the computer. Posting contributions by computer allows entry almost directly from the envelopes. The envelopes can be used in random order without being sorted either alphabetically or numerically. Usually the only preparation needed is to look up numbers for persons who gave without using their assigned envelopes and perhaps running a total on the contributions in a group of envelopes to be entered. This total is used as a cross check to ensure accuracy.

The fact that contributions can be entered without sorting envelopes speeds up the process of posting the gifts. It is also faster to use a numeric keyboard and enter an envelope number, fund number, and amount given than it would be to make manual entries on a form and have to handle the paper form for each contribution entered. With the computer the operator does no totaling and does not have to type up new contribution records at the beginning of each year. When it is time to produce quarterly statements, only a few keystrokes should be required to tell the machine to prepare the report from the data already entered.

More sophisticated church stewardship or giving software programs enable the system to do more than just record contributions. The software might allow the church to enter pledges the person has made. These pledges might be entered for multiple funds. For example, the person might pledge to give a certain amount to the regular operating budget and another amount to a building fund. With pledges entered it is possible to know if the amount given is consistent with the pledge.

Analyzing Giving

Having the capability to enter information in a computer always implies the ability to extract information. As noted, in the area of stewardship, this capability can be sensitive in many churches. Reports could be produced that gave the names of persons who had not given to the church budget for a given period. Similarly reports could tell who gave more than a set amount of money during the same period. It must be assumed that the church will provide its own safeguards on the records. The stewardship data should be protected by a password that is known only to those who are allowed access according to church policy. However, the capability for extracting information does give added possibilities for information management. Maintaining stewardship records is much faster and more accurate with a computer but more is possible than speeding up the existing process.

Often churches will print in newsletters a distribution of giving patterns. These will show the number of members who gave within certain ranges. A sample distribution produced by a stewardship software package is shown in Figure 4. This analysis allows a minister to look at giving patterns without looking at individual giving records. The contribution distribution can produce valuable information for a minister or church.

Figure 4. Contribution Distribution

BSST0303 1.03   Any Church   PAGE: 1
04/20/89   Contribution Distribution
                              01/01/88 thru 12/30/88

FUND: ** ALL CONTRIBUTIONS **

FROM		THRU	NUMBER
.00	–	.49	54
.50	–	.99	20
1.00	–	4.99	80
5.00	–	9.99	85
10.00	–	49.99	221
50.00	–	99.99	26
100.00	–	199.99	4
200.00	–	OVER	0

Average Weekly Gift for 490 Inidviduals $15.31

Figure 5. Thirty-two Week Contribution Distribution

Contribution Distribution

Range of Giving		Number Giving in This Range
From	To	
.01	.49	54
.50	.99	20
1.00	2.49	30
2.50	4.99	50
5.00	7.49	49
7.50	9.99	36
10.00	14.99	56
15.00	19.99	32
20.00	24.99	38
25.00	29.99	20
30.00	39.99	21
40.00	49.99	24
50.00	74.99	18

75.00	99.99	8
100.00	124.99	2
125.00	149.99	0
150.00	174.99	1
175.00	199.99	1
Total Number Giving		460

This distribution was used to estimate the overall giving of the congregation. During the period in question, 460 persons had given $286,000 to the church budget. Knowing that there were a total of 1035 resident church and Sunday School members it was estimated that 21 percent of the potential contributors to the church gave 81 percent of the gifts, and 55 percent of the potential contributors gave nothing to the regular church budget. The 55 percent figure was particularly disturbing. It was acknowledged that a certain percent of the families would give one gift for the entire family, but there was no reason to assume this made a major impact on the distribution.

Promoting Giving

Using a computer allows specific target groups to be identified and selected. A church that had done an analysis such as the one described earlier might determine that it needed to promote better giving. To do the promotion most effectively they might target such groups as:

(1) People who are not assigned offering envelopes.

(2) People who have not given.

(3) New members who joined after a major emphasis to promote giving had been completed.

With these groups selected the operator can produce lists, mailing labels, or other types of outputs to provide information for mail, telephone calls, or visits to the individuals. An example of such an effort would be to identify those who did not have offering envelopes. With the group identified, mailing labels might be produced to send a letter to each person who had not been assigned envelopes. The letter might come from the church financial secretary, church treasurer, church finance committee, or from the pastor. Such a letter might state the financial needs of the church, and indicate that for the convenience of the individual, an envelope number has been assigned and envelopes enclosed or sent separately. This procedure could be made much more personal by using the computer to print a personalized letter rather than using mailing labels. Printing personal letters requires the use of a word processing software package, which will be discussed in a later chapter.

Supporting a Stewardship Emphasis

Many churches usually have some type of financial campaign. Some churches have an annual emphasis to encourage members to make a pledge to the church budget. Another fund-raising campaign might raise capital for a new building. Different denominations and several private companies offer suggested budget subscription programs and/or capital programs that have proven successful. All of these efforts can involve the use of basic information that is kept on the computer. Capital fund-raising campaigns normally require a special committee to handle the accurate production of name and address lists for mailing and other uses. Having a computer with a member file already created would allow the campaign to be supported without requiring a special committee.

Often fund-raising programs will be much less successful than they should be simply because the church cannot provide the accurate name and address information needed to support the emphasis. From the discussion in the previous chapter, you will remember that the basic information used for stewardship records is the same data already entered and in use. The only addition has been recording gifts and pledges. The name, address, and phone number information has remained the same.

With the basic information already available, what can be done to support a contribution emphasis? Many budget subscription or financial campaigns involve some combination of the following: mailings to members, telephone calls, a rally or banquet, printed materials about the budget or about the proposed building, and visitation to homes of members. In some cases, the application involves using the computer to keep track of additional information during the progress of the campaign. For instance, if the church is planning a banquet, it would probably want to keep track of reservations and contact those who had not made them. In the same manner it would be possible to keep track of those who had made a pledge and follow-up to anyone who had not yet done so. Either type of record keeping would simply require entering a special code, flag, or profile on a member record.

Mailings to Members

There are two ways that member mailings can be done using the computer. These are: (1) print out mailing labels, and (2) prepare a "mail-merge" using word processing software in conjunction with membership software. The second procedure would allow the preparation of individually prepared, personal letters and envelopes. Mailing labels are faster, easier, and more widely used. The type of mailing depends on the purpose and intent of the piece to be mailed. Possible mailings might be: a mass mailing of the church budget, a personal letter soliciting a budget contribution, a special invitation to a banquet or rally, a thank you note for a contribution, an interim report showing result at the midpoint of the drive, or a report of the result of the campaign given.

Telephone Calls

Membership software can be used effectively to prepare lists to be given to persons to make phone calls. Phone calls might be made to schedule appointments for home visits, to take reservations for a banquet, or to encourage persons who had not yet made pledges. It is simple to prepare lists by family in an easy-to-read format. The list might be printed on one line or might be in a format that allowed room for notations. A church like the one mentioned above with about 1035 potential givers would probably have 400 to 600 family units. One printout could be done and separated into as many individual calling lists as needed. Twenty-five volunteer callers, each taking twenty family units, could contact 500 families. If the list were transferred to word processing it would be possible to have instructions for the callers printed directly on the list of persons to be called. The lists could be sorted in special ways if needed. Examples of special instructions, or *sort orders*, that might facilitate the calling include family unit, street address, visit area, Sunday School class, or by age.

Rally or Banquet

The primary use of the computer in planning a rally or banquet would be in sending invitations and making calls to confirm reservations. An effective use of the computer would be to flag those who had made reservations so that at a given point a list could be produced of those who had not yet planned to come. This would allow a final effort to enlist last minute sign-ups.

Printed Materials

The use of the computer to produce printed materials is almost endless. Chapter 8 on Word Processing will show some of the possibilities.

Home Visits

There are three major applications for the use of the computer in facilitating home visits: (1) sorting the names into groups to be visited, (2) preparing lists or cards to give the names and addresses of those to be visited, and (3) providing a means of recording the report of the visit.

Dividing a group of church families for the visitation effort can require a significant amount of work with manual records. A computer could sort the names and prepare a list or cards in practically the same step. The list of members could be sorted either by street address or by a user defined visit area code. A street address list would not include every person because a number of persons have post office boxes, but the list would still be a starting place. Codes for visit area would be as accurate as the church had assigned. With the list of persons to be visited defined and properly sorted, the needed information—family with head of house name, address, phone number, church relationship, and all family members' names might be printed on 3- by 5-inch or 4- by 6-inch cards. Church relationship is included because it is likely that there would be cases where a person was included for a stewardship visit that was not a member of the church. Other useful information might be marital status, date each person joined the church, and perhaps Christian education or Sunday School enrollment.

The cards would be printed and sorted into an approximate order for home visits. It is assumed here that the desired order would be geographic. If the cards were in a visit area order they would be ready for use. If they were in street order the operator might have to group them as needed. Groups of cards could be separated or combined to produce the correct number of families to give to a specific visitor. Again, stressing the flexibility of the computer, the cards might be sorted many different ways. For a particular campaign it could be desirable to have the visitors call on someone of their own age group. In such a case it would be just as easy to produce the same cards sorted by age.

With visitation underway, some type of report will be needed. It is tempting to keep information just because the information is there to keep. That is not wise. No report should be entered unless it has a purpose. The church might want to record completed visits so that a list of those not yet visited could be printed. In other situations there could be a need to record the result, such as a pledge made and perhaps the amount. Whatever the need, the software should provide a simple means of keeping the report.

A few points should be made about this and other general procedures using computer information. First, the computer will not make the calls or make the visits. A computer facilitates work. People still need to talk to people and visit with people. A second point is that as the information is used the data should improve. Information should be corrected as errors are found in phone numbers and addresses. New information should be added, such as names and birthdays of new children in the home. The same data base is being used, and the same data base is being updated for reuse. The third point to remember is the right of privacy and confidentiality. Information should never be given out that would violate the trust the individual has in the church. This applies to unlisted phone numbers or to information about giving. Each church will have to consider and decide what is proper information to keep on the system, what is proper information to provide to others, and how information is to be safeguarded. Safeguards to restrict data include:

• Passwords to limit access to all or specific portions of the system.

• Physical security in locking the system in an office if needed and knowing who has keys.

• Care in insuring that printouts containing sensitive data are protected.

What Should You Know about
Keeping up with What Is Given?

From what you have read in this chapter you should:

• Know that maintaining contribution records is an ideal use for computers in the church.

• Know that contribution software can enhance stewardship when used for analysis and in support of stewardship campaigns.

5

To Post or Not to Post Attendance

The use of attendance software provides a good contrast to stewardship software. Most churches already have someone keeping individual stewardship records. Computerizing the process should provide an immediate time-saving step and better availability of information. Churches typically do not keep attendance records beyond a head count in the classroom or a head count in the worship service. If the church decides to begin posting attendance on the computer it will probably mean adding a new job to the office routine. Anytime a new job is added, questions should be asked such as: why does this need to be done, what will be the advantages, will it be worth doing, and who will do the job?

To give a personal word, I used church software (membership, stewardship, outreach, and word processing) for four years without ever posting attendance and without ever feeling like I was missing something by not posting attendance. For two more years before leaving local church work, I added posting Sunday School attendance to what was being done on the computer and felt that it was well worth the effort. The first point to consider is that somebody has to do the posting. This means that someone, each week, has to sit at the keyboard and input the attendance. Whether it is Sunday School, choir, worship, communion, or any other church organization or function, someone has to do the entry.

Well-designed church software can keep a record of what activity every member participates in every week. The church or staff can decide if this type of member tracking needs to be done. **The most important question should be, do we need this information to further the outreach and ministry of our church?** It is possible to have someone spend a significant amount of time entering information that might be nice to have on occasion but will not be used enough to justify the time spent in entry. For some churches, keeping an accurate record of Sunday School attendance is important. Some churches keep records of attendance in training courses and award diplomas based on completion of courses. Other churches will want to carefully record worship attendance. What is to be kept and what is not kept becomes a local church decision, but it is an important decision because of the effort to be put into the attendance posting.

Four case studies of attendance posting should show the possibilities and how these possibilities add to the capabilities for information management.

Case 1

Church 1 registers the attendance of all persons in worship by passing clip boards down the pews during worship. Those attending write in their names. There is a column to check if you are a visitor. Worship attendance is the central activity of the church. Other activities such as Christian education, women's groups, and youth groups meet weekly, but the one activity for all church members is Sunday morning worship. Most of the contributions to the church come through the worship service.

If worship attendance were posted the church would immediately be able to identify members who are infrequent in attendance, chronic absentees, persons with perfect attendance, and other similar types of information. The typical means of posting attendance using church software is to set up the unit for posting attendance as an organization and to enroll members in it. This would mean creating an organization called "Church," "First Church," or "Grace Church," and then enrolling the members in the organization. Enrolling at this point is a slightly different procedure than the earlier discussion of a church relationship code. The church relationship code indicates actual membership status. Being a part of an organization for worship attendance is simply a convention to use for checking the attendance.

It would be possible and probably likely that there would be persons who would attend regularly and have attendance checked regularly that were not yet church members. Knowing that these persons were attending regularly, and knowing by their church relationship code that they were not yet church members would by itself be a very valuable piece of information for the pastor and other ministers.

The next step would be to gather the data on attendance. The means of doing this already exists. The church passes lists down each pew each Sunday. All persons are asked to sign their names. Visitors are asked to indicate by checking a column if they are visitors. How this information would be transferred to the computer could be a problem. The names would be completely random on separate random lists with no real way to be sorted. The operator might be able to post attendance by taking the random lists, retrieving each individual person's record, and then indicating that they were present for the Sunday in question.

Rather than post by going directly to each individual record, the operator should be able to record attendance by bringing up a list of all persons in the organization in question. Figure 6 shows an example used for posting attendance. Posting the names could be done in one of two ways. The attendance checklist would usually be alphabetical, and the data to be entered would obviously be in random order. To post the attendance directly from the random lists, the operator would move to each name on the checklist in the random order, for example, Payne, Turner, Brown, and North, and enter the attendance (perhaps Y for yes, or P for present). The other possibility would be to sort the names on the random lists so that the names would be alphabetical for faster posting.

The presorting could be done by an extra step, using word processing to sort the names. The procedure would be: (1) gather all random lists for a given Sunday, (2) use word processing and type all names in a simple manner only entering first name, last name, or first name, just as they are on the attendance sheets with each name on a new line, (3) sort the list alphabetically, and (4) print the sorted names. Assume the church had a large worship attendance of perhaps 1200. The 1200 names would represent 2400 words. Twelve hundred names could be retyped in about 30 to 60 minutes assuming 40 to 80 words per minute typing. Once the names were typed, the sorting would require only a minute or so, then the names could be printed, and the printout used for posting. For a smaller congregation the time would be much less. The church would have to decide if such a procedure facilitated data entry.

With a pre-sorted alphabetical list the names of those who attended would be in the same order as the list of the persons in the organization on the computer screen (Figure 6). At this point it would be a simple matter to move down the list and indicate Y for present.

Case 2

Church 2 has communion each week. Active member status, including voting in church meetings, depends on receiving communion; therefore, the church needs to record when each member has received communion. The procedure would be the same as for Church 1. An organization

Figure 6. Computer Screen Used For Posting Attendance

BSAT101A 1.08

9/19/89

Grace Baptist Church
Group Attendance Posting
Group ADU3-X46   Attendance Date 09/17/89

PERSON NO.	MEMBER NAME		PRESENT	VISITS	CONTACTS
000500-02	Andrews, Patricia J.	1.			
001500-01	Brown, Alvin	2.			
001500-02	Brown, Barbara	3.			
004200-02	Edwards, Marcia	4.			
006000-02	North, Julianne	5.			
007000-01	O'Malley, James	6.			
008500-02	Payne, Janet L.	7.			
008500-01	Payne, Robert R.	8.			
009000-01	Roberts, James	9.			
009000-02	Roberts, Joan	10.			
009500-01	Smithwick, Ralph W.	11.			
009500-02	Smithwick, Susan	12.			
009550-02	Turner, Mary	13.			

would be set up listing all persons who were eligible to take communion. The data for input would come from whatever means were used to register when communion was taken. If the registration could be done by having the persons check a preprinted list with their name on it, then the sorting would already be done. If cards were filled out, they could be sorted, and if a sign up list were used, it could be sorted as in the previous example.

If a church posted communion and also posted separately their worship attendance, it would be possible to identify easily those who were attending worship but were not taking communion. The access to data remains the key factor in the capability being made available with the computer.

Case 3

Church 3 has an active Sunday School program. They desire to keep accurate attendance records by member to contact absentees, recognize outstanding attendance, and allow analysis of the organization for future growth and restructuring. Some churches use the Sunday School as a primary organization. In such churches, active church members, adults as well as children, will be enrolled in a Sunday School class. The Sunday School is often used as a mechanism for church growth and evangelism. In such a situation, a structured organization will develop and the accuracy of the Sunday School enrollment and attendance records can be important to the work of the church.

A structured Sunday School organization would have not only classes but classes as a part of departments and departments making up age-group divisions. A Sunday School with 600 members might easily have twenty-five or thirty classes, and these classes might be in eight to twelve different departments. To maintain such an organization the software should be capable of supporting a multilevel organizational structure. The Sunday School organization would be set up as supported by the software. The software should produce some type of attendance checklist that would then be given to the classes on a weekly basis for checking attendance. A sample check list is shown in Figure 7.

When posting Sunday School using attendance software the procedure would be as follows:

(1) Set up the Sunday School organization as allowed by the software being used.

Figure 7. Attendance Checklist

BSAT0201 1.03   PAGE: 1
04/26/89

Grace Baptist Church
Attendance Checklist – Sunday School
04/26/89

Group Identification AD01-C18 Adult 1 (18-29)   Coed 18-29

Announcements

1) There will be an all church fellowship tonight after the evening service.   2) Support the youth. Stop by their car wash Saturday.

PERSON NO	NAME	CH REL	LAST ATTEND	PRES-ENT	VIS-ITS	CON-TACTS	PERSON NO	NAME	CH REL	LAST ATTEND	PRES-ENT	VIS-ITS	CON-TACTS
	** MEMBERS **												
1500-11	Brown, Kim	A		___	___	___							
1500-12	Brown, Kristine	S		___	___	___							
3800-02	Cunningham, Debra	A		___	___	___							
4300-02	Gregory, Ann	A		___	___	___							
5000-01	Harper, Raymond	A		___	___	___							
5900-01	Neighbours, David	S		___	___	___							
5900-02	Neighbours, Pamela	S		___	___	___							
7500-02	Patton, Sara	S		___	___	___							
9500-11	Smithwick, Donald	A		___	___	___							
	** PROSPECTS **												
2000-02	Brown, Linda	B		___	___	___							
7400-02	Ohning, Donna	P		___	___	___							
7400-01	Ohning, Joel	P		___	___	___							
9750-02	Wallace, Cindy	B		___	___	___							
9750-01	Wallace, James	P		___	___	___							

Total Enrolled 10

** Period Totals ** Enrolled members present _____   New members present _____   Visitors present _____   Total present _____

Total visits made _____   Total other contacts _____   Total contributions _____

(1) Turn in visitor's cards on all guests.   (2) Be sure any absent members are given a call this week.

(2) Print attendance checklists for the next Sunday and distribute the lists to the classes.

(3) Classes check the attendance and return the lists.

(4) At some time in the next week the attendance is posted and new checklists are printed and distributed.

Several things are important about the use of such a checklist.

(1) It should be possible to have the software produce all checklists for the entire Sunday School organization with one procedure.

(2) The attendance checklist shown has several useful features:

• It gives the date the person last attended which provides an immediate flag to the teacher if someone begins to miss.

• It provides some space at both the top and bottom of the checklist to make announcements and give special instructions. This extra means of communicating with each class each week can be very useful.

• Prospective members assigned to the class can be listed on the attendance checklist.

(3) Note again the use of the church relationship codes. Some of the Sunday School members are resident church members enrolled in Sunday School (A), and some are Sunday School members only (S). In the same manner some of the prospective Sunday School members are prospects (P), and some are resident church members not enrolled in Sunday School (B).

Case 4

Church 4 has a well organized and growing choir program for all ages. They want to post attendance by choir for both rehearsals and performances. Awards and recognitions are given based on participation.

Posting attendance in this instance would be similar to what was done to post Sunday School attendance. The first requirement would be to create the organizational structure and enroll the persons in the appropriate choir. If an extensive choir program was needed the software would have to be capable of showing multiple enrollments within one organization. For example, one person might be: (1) an adult choir member, (2) a handbell choir member, (3) a special ensemble member, and (4) a children's choir worker. The software needs to be capable of handling the basic participation of the average member and also allow record keeping for the smaller percent of members who are involved in many functions.

In this example, one person would need to be enrolled in four different music groups. Once enrolled, his or her attendance would be posted weekly for all four groups. Posting of attendance could be done in the same manner as the posting of Sunday School. Attendance checklists could be prepared for all groups for each week and then checklists returned for data entry.

The Use of Attendance Data

These four church situations represent four different needs for posting attendance and give suggestions for how the attendance might be kept. Assuming the records were kept week by week what might be the result? The following are different types of information that the software should be capable of producing for the pastor, staff, or lay leadership in the church or organizations:

(1) Persons with perfect attendance in worship, communion, Sunday School, or choirs.

(2) Chronic absentees or persons who have not attended in months.

(3) Persons who have begun to miss (absent the last three Sundays).

(4) Persons regularly attending church or Sunday School, or persons participating in a choir who are not yet church members.

(5) Persons attending church but not taking communion.

(6) Numbers of total people attending. Often churches deal with total membership and average attendance. For example, a church might have 700 members and average 325 in Sunday worship. However, if the records could be checked they might find that 500 members attend at least one Sunday a month or twelve times a year.

(7) Number of people attending regularly. This is a similar figure to total in attendance. If the church defined regular attendance as being present nine of thirteen Sundays in a quarter then it would be possible to see how many persons met this standard and who they were.

(8) Attendance of workers. Occasionally a problem will arise in that workers do not attend regularly. Attendance software would allow the staff or leadership to check the attendance of those who have agreed to serve as teachers or other workers.

(9) Statistical data by organization. The attendance software should produce information on total membership, number of visitors, number of new members, and average attendance for specified periods such as a month, quarter, or year.

The use of the information becomes the task of the pastor, staff, and lay leadership. Combining checking attendance with membership data opens up many possibilities. When age, sex, or marital status is combined with attendance information the church can have an accurate picture of the congregation to answer such questions as:

- Do we have younger members or older members actively attending?
- Are our youth participating?
- Do we have single adults participating?

It must be stressed that there is a price for this type of information. The price is: (1) having software that will accomplish the work, (2) having the organizations set up to allow the attendance to be posted, (3) providing the means to gather the attendance data, (4) perhaps most importantly, having a person who will do the actual posting each week, and (5) having the imagination to make use of the information if it is posted.

One extra advantage comes with posting attendance, particularly for a churchwide organization such as for Sunday School or worship. This advantage is the enforced regular discipline of checking records. We all pay monthly bills. On most all return envelopes there will be a question that says, "Is this a change of address?" with a box to check *yes* or *no*. Insurance companies, mortgage companies, and other businesses know they must strive to keep their records correct. Churches need to learn to do the same thing. If Sunday School attendance is posted using attendance checklists printed by the computer, then the result is that the church makes a 100 percent check of the Sunday School roll by name each week. If a person is in the wrong class, not enrolled when they should be, or not dropped from the roll, the errors should be quickly found. Other types of errors could be caught through attendance checking. It is easy to forget to update records when someone marries or divorces, and a name changes. These types of errors could be noticed during attendance checking and quickly corrected.

What Should You Know about Posting Attendance?

From what you have read in this chapter you should:

- Know that posting attendance requires someone to enter attendance records each week.
- Understand that posting attendance significantly enhances the ability to manage information.

6

Outreach: What PCs Are Made to Do

Churches seek to spread their message. In different places and in different denominations, how the message is spread takes different forms. Churches seek to grow, or at least the topic of growing is a part of church work. Churches in the United States grew rapidly in the 1950s but many declined in the 60s and 70s. During the late 1970s and 80s, attention has been given to what has been called the Church Growth Movement. The Church Growth Movement focuses on the need for churches to show definite numerical increase in membership and conversions. While the Church Growth Movement has been key in some denominations, others have used Sunday School as the primary means for outreach, growth, and evangelism.

Outreach means the process of identifying prospective members, maintaining information about the prospects, furnishing that information to church members to make contacts to the prospects, and then receiving reports to update the information on file and continue the process. Outreach would normally be done to bring non-church members into the church or enroll new members in a Sunday School. Efforts might also be made within the church fellowship to enlist persons in a choir or to increase the participation in other church activities or organizations.

Whatever type of outreach might be planned or needed, the computer provides the ideal means of supporting the work. It could be argued that no large-scale outreach program can be supported without some means of record keeping like that provided by the computer. Obviously churches reached people for twenty centuries without the use of computers. However, it is also obvious that the church today exists in a different world than it did in the previous nineteen centuries. People are extremely mobile. The parish church where a given church served a specific community and the pastor knew all of the residents no longer exists. Small community churches find themselves surrounded by booming suburban areas. Downtown churches find their communities changing. Achieving some degree of control over what is going on in a church field is difficult at best.

The problems involved in outreach can be made clearer with an example. Assume a church of about 400 members averages about 150 to 225 in worship attendance. The church is located in what has been a stable community, but due to new job opportunities the community is now seeing a steady increase in new families. Three to five new families or single adults visit the worship service each week. Visitor cards are given out and usually completed and returned. The staff consists of a full-time pastor, part-time secretary, and part-time music minister.

In such a situation, the pastor might send a personal note or letter to each new visitor and try to call or visit the following week. The visitor's cards would accumulate in a file box. In twelve to eighteen months, 100 to 200 cards could build up in the box. While the pastor would be concerned about the visitors, he would also know that with 400 members and about half that number attending worship he would also have a significant number of inactive members to be concerned with. The pastor might also have some nagging feeling that even though new persons were visiting each week, there were other newcomers in the community that were not visiting the church and should be contacted and invited to attend.

This example points out at least three groups that are targets for outreach: new visitors, inactive members, and persons in the community not attending any church. There are many factors that affect outreach, including the attitude of the church toward growth. Theology, commitment, church polity, and this chapter assumes that the church and pastor have made the decision to either begin to do outreach or improve the outreach being done. The chapter shows what the computer offers to support the work.

One simple illustration common to most ministers will explain the value of a computer in the area of outreach. Almost every pastor has stood in the pulpit at least once and said, "If every one of you will go home and call a friend then our building will be full for our revival, choir special, Easter drama, special service, and so forth." The appeal is made in all sincerity, and in fact if everyone did as asked the building would be full. The problem is that the calls do not get made. If they were made, probably a few people would get duplicate calls, and most of the calls would be to regularly attending, but temporarily absent, church members.

A better appeal, much more likely to produce results, would be:

> Would you be willing to call one person this week and invite them to our special service? If you would, as you leave church this morning see me, and I will give you a 3- by 5-inch card with the name, telephone number, and address of someone to call. There will be a note on the card as to when they last visited our church and their denominational preference. If we know of other family members, their names will be on the card also.

It is not hard to determine why such appeals are seldom made, considering the normal state of information on prospective members. If the best information consists of random visitor's cards, sorted by the date visited if sorted at all, then it is really impossible to produce cards quickly for distributing to members. If, however, the basic information is on a computer, then the needed cards can be produced in minutes.

The basic purpose in keeping information on prospective members should be to use that information to contact the prospects contacted and invite them to church. These contacts should occur in a variety of ways, including personal mail, mass mail, telephone calls, and personal visits. The contacts need to come from a variety of persons, including the pastor, staff, deacons, Sunday School teachers, and other laypersons in the church. **There is no better or more effective way to have calls and contacts made than to have the information on a computer.** With the computer, as has been shown, significant information can be selected quickly and easily. Once selected, the information can be produced in a variety of printed forms to give to members for action. With the computer, the minister can seek to provide prospective member names to a lot of persons in a lot of different means for multiple types of contacts. As contacts are made, further efforts can be made to receive reports, refine the information on the prospects, and seek to make more effective contacts in the future.

Prospect Information

It would be helpful to look at what information might be kept on prospects. As indicated in the chapter on membership software, the most basic data consists of: name, address, phone number, birthday, sex, and marital status. The titles Mr., Mrs., Miss, Ms., Dr., and so forth would be an additional field of information related to sex and marital status. A prospect software package should allow the church to also keep several additional pieces of information. Possible additional fields are listed as follows:

Prospect Date	The date the person became a prospect and was added to the computer.
Date Visited	The most recent date the prospect visited the church.
Source	The source the name came from, for instance, the person might have visited the church or the name might have come from Welcome Wagon or a tip from a member.
Church Preference	The person's denominational preference or background. It would be expected that not all prospects would be of the same denomination as the church they were visiting. Some might express no preference.
Follow-up Date	A date assigned when the person is to be contacted again.
Date Contacted	The date contacts have been made with the prospect.
Contact Type	Whether a contact with the prospect was a telephone call, home visit or perhaps a contact by the pastor or a lay person in the church.
Result of Contact	Some means should be provided to indicate the results of contacts with the prospect. This might be done through codes for different types of responses or by typing information in a notes field describing the visit or call.

With this information entered for all persons that the church considers prospective members, many opportunities become possible. A minister might get any of the following lists:

- Persons who visited the church within the last month, three months, six months, and so forth.
- Persons who have visited the church but have not received a personal call or visit from the pastor or other ministers.

- Persons who are listed as prospects who are of either the same or different denominational preference from the church. A change in denominational preference here might indicate that newcomers to the community tended to be of different denominational backgrounds than the local persons.
- Persons who are supposed to receive follow-up contacts this week.
- Persons who are listed as prospects but have never actually visited the church.
- Persons who have been listed as prospects for over twelve, eighteen, and twenty-four months.

Combining the basic data with the additional prospect data creates even more possibilities. For instance, any of the above selections could be sorted by sex, age, or marital status. A youth leader might be interested in teenage boys who have visited recently.

A particular problem with prospect records can be missing or incomplete information. Much of the special prospect data, as listed earlier, will be generated by the church and will be as accurate and complete as the church reports and records. Basic data on prospects, however, will often be sketchy. A typical visitors card might give the following information:

Lynn Jones
120 Oak Park, Nashville, Tennessee 32322
343-1111

With this data, answer the following questions:
- How old is Lynn?
- Is Lynn a Mr., Mrs., Ms., or Miss?
- Is Lynn married or single?

Another card might read:

Mr. and Mrs. Lynn Jones
120 Oak Park, Nashville, Tennessee 32322
343-1111

Here it is safe to assume that Lynn is a married man, but age and his wife's name are still missing, and you might wonder if there are children in the family.

The fact that these problems exist should never deter a church from using the computer for outreach. Some simple solutions to the problem of missing information exist. First, visitors cards can be worded to allow the visitor to enter titles, age ranges, children's names, and so forth. Second, if someone will call the person and have a brief, casual, and nonprobing phone conversation, he or she will probably be able to fill in much of the missing information. Even if data is incomplete, considerable valuable information is still present that can be used for contacting prospects. The user would be advised to enter accurately what is available and use what is present but not to guess and attempt to enter unknown data. For example, entering a title of Miss when the person happens to be a 75-year-old widow or entering a sex of male and a title of Mr. when the person is a woman who prefers Ms. could be embarrassing errors.

An Outreach Plan

In comparing the kinds of software discussed so far, the following conclusion can be reached. All of the software modules require and assume accurate data, but the application and use of the data differs. Membership data will not be used unless someone deliberately seeks to use the information and uses his or her imagination and creativity in extracting and printing information in usable forms. Use of stewardship data requires 100 percent accurate data entry, but the primary application is fixed because of the need for printing stewardship reports for members for tax returns. Use of attendance data requires someone to update attendance records weekly, and someone needs to show imagination in how to put the data to use. Prospect information differs from any of these other three church computer uses. Prospect software requires accurate data but the data is certain to be more incomplete than in other areas and may be less accurate. Use of the data requires some imagination, but imagination alone is not enough.

Effective use of prospect software requires something not a part of other software use. It needs an ongoing plan to put the potential of the software to use. The plan should cover receiving names from various sources, entering data, assigning persons for contacts, furnishing information to those who will make contacts, receiving reports, updating data, and recirculating the information for follow-up contacts. The need to furnish information to other persons for action (contacts) and the requirement to receive reports makes a plan necessary. As reports are received, data is updated and more effective future contacts are made.

Consider this situation: A church has from two to ten visiting families each week. The visitors are a mix of husband, wife, and children; couples without children; singles; and single parents. Most visitors fill out a visitor card on at least their first visit. Some will fill out a second or third card on subsequent visits. The visitor card used by a church is shown in Figure 8. In some cases each family member fills out a card completely, and in other cases only one member will complete a card for the entire family. The names of spouse and children may or not be included. The pastor is concerned because only a fraction of the visitors continue to attend and unite with the church. Out of ten to forty new families visiting each month, one to three families may join the church. There are far too many visitors for the pastor to give personal attention to each visitor and still do all other needed duties.

Figure 8. Sample Visitor Card

Mr.
Mrs.
Miss   Name   Date
Ms.
Address _____
Phone _____
I am a guest of: _____
Church Member   Yes   No
What Church _____
  Age 1-5 6-11 12-17 18-29 30-39 40-49 50-59 60-69 70-99

The pastor needs help with the task of contacting and welcoming new visitors. With cards coming in, the plan can begin. The pastor believes that the following actions would contribute significantly to the welcoming of visitors and the outreach of the church:

(1) A personal letter to each new family on Monday morning after their first visit to the church.

(2) A personal telephone call from a church member or minister expressing appreciation for having the family in church and inviting them back. This call needs to be made on Thursday or Friday after the visit.

(3) A second personal telephone call from a church member or minister during the second week after the visit.

Further actions to contact the person will be determined by the results of the three contacts and interest shown by the family in the church. It is felt that if this much can be done on a regular basis, then it would be a significant improvement in the overall outreach of the church. A group of volunteers can be recruited to make the telephone calls. The intent is to mix the calls so that one will come from a minister and one will be from a layperson. An outreach plan could be outlined as follows:

(1) Visitor cards will be given to the church secretary or volunteer who will enter the names into the computer with address and phone number by 10:00 a.m. on Monday morning. The Sunday date will be entered as a prospect date and as the date the person visited the church. Titles, church preference, spouse and children's names, ages, birthdays, and other information will be entered if known.

(2) A word processing merge list will be created as soon as names are entered for the new visitors. This merge list will be used with the sample letter in Figure 9 to prepare personal letters to all new visitors. Letters will be edited as needed to personalize salutations. These letters will be mailed on Monday. Chapter 8 on word processing will discuss merge functions.

Figure 9. Letter to New Visitors

Dear (prospect's name to be inserted),

It was a pleasure to have you in our worship service this past Sunday. Whether you are new to our community or have lived here for sometime, we offer our church to you as a place of worship and fellowship. You will find that we care about you. There is a place for you in our Sunday School (Bible study) that meets at 9:45 on Sunday morning. In addition to Sunday School, we have choir, youth activities, mission groups, and much more.

We hope you will visit again soon. If you need any assistance or have questions about our church feel free to give me a call at any time.

Sincerely,

Pastor

(3) As soon as the letters are complete, 3- by 5-inch cards will be printed for the new visitors with one card for each family. Each family card will be stapled to an information sheet (Figure 10) that gives instructions for calling, what to say, and requests for information to be reported to the church. Callers will be trained to make calls in a friendly, welcoming manner and to pick up information conversationally. The calls should not sound like surveys. Callers are to receive their cards and instructions by Wednesday and make the calls on Thursday or Friday.

(4) The pastor will go through the cards before they are distributed and select those he (or another minister) will call. The ministers will also complete the information sheet for the person they call.

(5) All cards with information sheets are to be returned by the next Sunday. When the cards are returned, the prospect record will be updated with any new data from the information sheet, the date of the contact, type of contact (layperson or staff), and pertinent results.

(6) When information sheets are returned, a telephone list is made for new prospects, and a second telephone list will be prepared for prospects who received a telephone call the previous week. There will be two groups in this list. One group will be those persons who received their first call from the staff person, and the second group will be those who received their first call from a layperson. When the second call is made, there should not be any need to get information, assuming the first call was successful and correctly done. The second call would have several purposes (1) to show the person that the church cared enough to have both a minister and a layperson call, (2) encourage the person or family to visit again, and (3) get an indication of the person's level of interest so further follow-up can be planned if needed. The person making the second call would return the card the following Sunday with any notes, information, or comments written on the card. Based on the result of the second call a decision could be made about keeping the person as a prospect and when and how to continue to follow-up the outreach.

Figure 10. Outreach Information Sheet

Please call the person/family on the attached card before next Sunday. When you call you should:

(1) Introduce yourself by name and as being from Grace Church.

(2) Give them a warm welcome and thank them for coming to worship with us.

(3) Seek to add to or clarify the information we have. We do not want the person to feel they are being questioned or examined.

The following questions should sound normal and non-threatening. It is not necessary to ask questions when the information is on the card.

- What is your spouse's name?
- What are your children's names, and what grades are they in?
- What is your church background?

Without asking, but from the conversation, you should have an idea about the following information: sex, marital status, and age.

Thanks for your help. Your call lets a visitor know we care. The information you return helps us to continue to reach out and minister.

In this situation described, a plan such as the one outlined should be a significant help to the church. All visitors would be acknowledged though both a letter and personal phone calls. The phone calls should produce additional information on visitors to help the pastor, outreach minister, or a lay leader guide further outreach. Many other things could be added to an outreach plan. Many churches have active home visitation programs. Other churches have active personal evangelism emphases that involve home visits. Either type of outreach could be supported in a manner similar to what was done with the telephone calls.

A church that keeps active and up-to-date prospect information would find other uses for the data. For example, many churches have annual special events such as revivals or holiday programs at Easter, Christmas, Thanksgiving, or Independence Day. These events are excellent opportunities to invite prospective members to attend. With the information in the computer, it would be easy to send special invitations or tickets with a note worded to appeal to the person being invited. Prospects could easily be assigned to Sunday School classes for ongoing outreach efforts. Some church software will have special provisions for assigning prospects to Sunday School classes.

Another use of the ability to keep prospect information is to extend the church's outreach beyond its own members and those who come to visit. Churches and ministers are painfully aware that a large segment of the population simply does not go to church. This group is in the community but will not visit or attend special services. Unless the church finds them, they will never be reached. Reaching this part of the community may require door-to-door visitation or telephone surveys to identify the unchurched. Once the unchurched are identified, they must be contacted and invited to attend in appropriate, non-threatening ways. What prospect software provides is the ability to manage the information even in large numbers.

In one rapidly growing area of Georgia, a number of churches joined together to do a telephone survey of several thousand homes. The results of the survey were entered on a computer in the associational office. Once entered the data was available to any church. One church asked for the names of persons in its local zip codes who had indicated that either they had no local church affiliation or seldom attended any local church. That church received over 1,000 names, though the other information was sketchy. In most cases all that was known was name, address, and telephone number. However knowing that much and knowing that there was no local church affiliation, it was possible to begin making efforts to contact the people. The computer facilitated handling the names so that they could be assigned to visitation teams or assigned to volunteers to telephone and get more information.

Many churches are now using various services to receive lists of newcomers to their area. These lists come on computer printouts with name, address, and telephone number. Outreach software provides the ideal means of getting these new names to church members or into a planned program of personal mail to insure that new residents are invited to attend.

Churches seeking to grow and reach people today face two critical obstacles that can be overcome with the aid of a computer. The first is that the time church members have available to give is a limited and precious resource. The computer can facilitate providing the best information, in an easy to use form, on persons that need to be contacted by individuals. This makes the work of doing outreach as easy as possible. The second obstacle is that in a mobile, active, changing society where people are on the move and often not at home, keeping up with persons is difficult. It is easy for the name of a visitor to get misplaced before anyone contacts the individual. When contact is made, the report may never get back for follow-up. The only real solution is to effectively use computer software so that names are kept and outreach to persons can be tracked and monitored.

The computer will not make calls or give a warm smile and friendly greeting to a visitor at the door. Persons must do that. The computer will help churches that want to reach people do the work more effectively.

What Should You Know about
Using Computers in Outreach?

From what you have read in this chapter you should:

● Realize that use of prospect records must allow for missing or incomplete information.

● Be able to formulate an outreach plan that makes effective use of information provided by outreach software.

7

Accounting: What Do You Want to Know?

Most ministers do not want to know about debits, credits, charts of accounts, and "assets equal liabilities plus capital." Ministers normally are concerned with accounting in the sense of "do we have enough money in the bank to pay our bills?" Or "can we afford to go ahead and do all the things we budgeted to do this year?" In discussing church applications for accounting software, two things need to be considered.

First, accounting software is a different application from the stewardship software discussed in chapter 4, and the two normally do not tie together. With stewardship software, the church keeps a record of contributions from members, primarily to furnish members statements of giving for tax purposes. Stewardship software also has other major uses such as keeping up with pledges, analyzing giving, and promoting giving. Accounting software has a different function. **Accounting software keeps up with the church books. Once the Sunday offering has been counted and the money separated from the offering envelopes, accounting software is ready to go into action.** The envelopes or list of names of those who gave, with amounts given, go the person who will post giving. The offering is deposited in the bank and deposit slips showing where the funds were deposited and total amounts deposited to different funds go to the person who keeps the books. The person may or may not be the same person who posts the stewardship records.

The ability to manage information is the second point to consider. The basic theme of this book is that computers allow ministers to manage information in order to facilitate, support, and carry out the outreach and ministry of the local church. How does this apply to the area of accounting? Accounting records or church financial records differ from member and prospect records. While manually-maintained member records are often inaccurate and the data contained in the records inaccessible, typically manual accounting records are accurate, and information is regularly available. To say information is regularly available means that on a routine schedule (usually monthly) reports are submitted. Information may or may not be readily available at other times. Accounting records are better kept for a fairly simple reason. For a church to operate and conduct business, income in the form of gifts and offerings must be deposited, and salaries and bills paid. In addition, most congregations expect a full accounting of funds to be made. A church must have someone, either volunteer or paid, keeping up with the money.

A common practice is to have a finance committee, a treasurer, and perhaps a financial secretary responsible for the church's money. Either the treasurer or the financial secretary keeps the books and writes the checks. A monthly financial report shows income and expenses, often in terms of a line-item budget. A portion of a typical, manually produced financial statement is shown in Figure 11. Information reported will vary from church to church, but in this case for each budget item the four columns report: annual budgeted amount (Budget), amount spent for the month (Month), total amount spent for the year (To Date), and the balance for that item (Balance). The budgeted amount indicates how much the church planned or expected to spend in a certain area. Actual amounts spent for each budget item or account are reported for the period (usually a month) and for the year-to-date. A figure in parentheses in the *Balance* column would indicate that the church had overspent what was budgeted for that item. The church may fall behind in relation to the budget by either not having enough income from offerings to cover the expected expenses, by overspending in certain areas, or by spending for projects or items not planned in the budget.

The information the minister needs on financial matters is basic and simple. The minister or church leader needs to know if the income is sufficient to meet the overall budget and if spending is going as expected so that money is available for each budgeted item. For example, the music minister would want to know if he or she had enough money remaining to purchase materials for Christmas music. In most budgets a large amount of the money is inflexible. Salaries, utilities, debt retirement, telephone bills, and other such things must be paid. Fixed expense items may make up 70 percent or more of the overall budget. If the church is running behind in giving by 10 percent then the difference must come from those items that can be put off or cut back. These might be amounts of literature ordered, fellowship-type activities, purchase of new equipment

Figure 11. Manual Financial Statement

Financial Statement
August 1995

Organizational and Educational Ministries

	Budget	Month	To Date	Balance
Sunday School	6,500.00	1,739.59	5,101.53	1,398.47
Vacation Bible School	400.00	68.26	674.88	(274.88)
Woman's Missionary Union	1,400.00	54.49	202.47	1,197.53
Music Literature	4,933.00	473.71	2,005.82	2,927.18
Church Media Center	400.00	81.85	288.37	11.63
Youth Program	1,500.00	195.62	1,278.10	221.90
Training	1,500.00	80.17	1,229.74	270.26
Baptismal Supplies	50.00	0.0	0.0	50.00
Bus Expense	1,300.00	313.96	852.57	447.73

Service Ministries

	Budget	Month	To Date	Balance
Printing	6,000.00	507.94	4,434.13	1,565.87
Postage and Office Supplies	1,500.00	391.37	3,971.91	528.09
Offering Envelopes	1,000.00	0.0	489.58	510.42
Church Flowers	300.00	0.0	26.00	274.00
Food Services	1,200.00	190.01	1,872.40	(672.40)

Building Maintenance

	Budget	Month	To Date	Balance
Water, Lights, & Gas	11,000.00	1,097.52	8,249.85	2,750.15
Telephone	4,000.00	409.03	2,986.20	1,013.80
Insurance	4,000.00	343.00	2,967.41	1,032.59
Fuel	12,000.00	0.0	10,035.32	1,964.68
Janitorial & Kitchen Supplies	1,500.00	119.88	775.72	724.28
Repair and Maintenance	12,250.00	0.0	11,871.92	378.08

(like computers), or mission giving. Since there are always more good and important things that need to be done than there is money, attention to how money is budgeted and actually spent is important.

Some ministers take an absolute, hands off, "its not my concern, let the finance committee watch over the money," attitude. This minister only wants to know when there isn't enough money for a given project. This doesn't mean the person with this attitude might not be concerned about the giving of the members. He just doesn't feel it is his responsibility to keep track of details about the money. Other ministers want to know where every dollar goes and what every check is written for. This type of minister may even want to screen checks before they are signed or sign them himself. This person may or may not be concerned about the mechanics of how the books are kept, but he does want to know in detail where the funds go.

If a church already receives a manually produced financial report each month that is accurate and up-to-date, why use a computer? **Accounting software adds: (1) greater accuracy and less error, (2) more efficiency with more up-to-date information, and (3) vastly improved reporting procedures.** A case study will be used to illustrate how each of these three points might affect a local church.

Let's consider a church with 900 members and a budget of $300,000 per year. Its five-person staff consists of a pastor, minister of music, two full-time secretaries, and a full-time custodian. They routinely write 70 to 100 checks per month. Giving in relation to budgeted needs for the last several years has varied from 90 percent to 105 percent of what is required. Records have been maintained manually. The finance committee receives a financial report for the previous month on the first Wednesday of each month. The monthly financial statement is presented to the church on the second Wednesday in a business session.

With the growth of the church budget and expansion of the staff in recent years, the part-time financial secretary has a difficult time keeping stewardship records up-to-date and maintaining the books properly. Years ago the church kept two bank accounts, one for savings and one for checking. Today they keep special funds in certificates of deposit and money market accounts. These must be monitored to get the best interest rates. Additional staff has meant more payroll and tax work. With a much more complicated set of finances, typically the first week of each month involves a frenzy of activity to get the previous month closed out so a report can be prepared. The monthly financial statement is seldom ready for the finance committee meeting. A verbal or partial report is made to the committee and a printed report done in time for the church conference. Books are kept accurately, but the secretary rarely has time to give the ministers information they might need. If a minister wants to know how much money is available for church literature, the secretary must try to remember what bills have come in that might not have been paid yet and then go to the ledger and do a quick total of that account since the last financial statement. **In a manual system, putting the information into a report requires a major effort that involves totaling and cross-checking. When the books don't balance, hours may be spent in finding where a credit or debit was incorrectly posted.**

A full church accounting package allows the church to put all accounting functions on the computer system. All bank accounts, savings accounts, and certificates would be entered. The full church budget would be listed. A report would be provided to include all designated funds and allow additional designated funds to be added. The system would maintain a list of all vendors that the church did business with and allow bills due to be posted for later payment. The church payroll would be done by the system and would include figuring income taxes, social security, and keeping up with other deductions for such things as annuity or hospitalization. Both payroll and vendor checks could be printed by the system. If the church received income from rents or other sources or maintained trust funds these could be kept in the system. If it were desired to maintain a school or other entity as a separate set of books, it could be done with the same software.

Greater Accuracy

Accounting software provides greater accuracy and less error. Ideally, the books would be set up so that any financial transaction was handled with only one entry, and any accounts affected by the transaction were automatically credited or debited as appropriate. This is exactly what a good software package provides. The phrase "when the books are set up" is important. Any system will require work in getting the books arranged to correctly reflect the financial picture of the church. Once this is done however it should be possible to handle transactions with only one entry in the books and to get any needed report. Since the system does all the math and cross referencing of transactions, much of the error that occurs in a manual system will be eliminated.

Better Efficiency

Accounting software offers more efficiency with more up-to-date information. The increased efficiency and availability of more up-to-date information from accounting software can be explained by showing how some typical transactions might be entered and what information might then be available.

For example, *Transaction 1:* The telephone bill for June comes on July 5 payable by July 17. With an accounts payable function in the accounting software, this transaction would be entered immediately. The operator would go to the account set up for the telephone company and would indicate that a bill or invoice was due to be paid on a certain date. The entry would probably include the date, a reference number for the bill, a description column for something like "June Phone Bill," and the name of the account the money was to be charged against. This entry would require less time than it would take to write or type a check and then post the check in a journal or register.

In most cases the church would have an item in the budget for telephone expenses. If the accounting package operated in real time, then as soon as the entry was made in accounts payable, the telephone account would be charged with the bill, even if the check was not yet written. This would mean that if a minister asked how much was spent for telephone and the secretary knew that all bills were entered, then this amount would have been charged against the phone budget and the information on amount spent would be accurate. When it came time to write the checks the secretary would put checks into the computer printer, go into accounts payable, and indicate that vendors who had checks due to be paid by a certain date should now have checks written. The system would probably want to know the starting check number and the date to go on the check. A command would be given to start the printing. The system would credit or debit any accounts affected. For instance, the bank account would be reduced by the amount of the check and the amount spent for telephone for the the year would be increased.

Transaction 2: The bill arrives for church literature from the denominational publishing house. The total is $2,342.00. The money must be charged to several different line items in the budget, including Sunday School and music ministry.

This would probably be handled as the phone bill was done above; however, in this case the invoice covers several accounts. It should be possible to write one check and make one entry in the system but indicate in the system that the amount of the check is to be charged to, or distributed over, several different budget items. Charging the bank account with the expenditure and charging the amount spent to a budget line item occur as each transaction is entered. At any point a balanced financial report can be produced. Different software packages do have different characteristics. Some packages require accounting periods, such as months, be closed out before reports can be generated, but it is possible to buy software that allows up-to-date reports at any time.

Transaction 3: A gift was received in the form of a check designated to be used for the purchase of a new piano. Designated funds are a normal part of church accounting. Some churches have strict policies on what can be excepted in the form of designated gifts, and there are tax implications for individuals on what and how they give designated funds. Churches will have persons who designate their gift to be used for a particular purpose. The manner in which designated funds are kept may vary considerably. Some churches might place all funds in one checking account and keep track of what amount of the total is general budget money and what amount is designated for various purposes. Others may keep one bank account for budget money and another account for all designated funds. Another approach is to have separate bank accounts for each designated gift. Whatever the physical disposition of the funds in various bank accounts, the gift mentioned above would be deposited in the proper account with the deposit going in the books as being credited to the appropriate designated fund. Looking at the account on the computer would show the fund balance at any time.

Improved Reporting Procedures

Accounting software provides significant improvements in reporting.[1] Another capability of the software is the ability to specify the information to be displayed on a financial statement. Figures 12 and 13 show two different reports for the same section of a church budget. Figure 12 provides a much more detailed accounting of the funds than is given in the report shown in Figure 13. Figure 13 shows the same columns of information as were given on the manually produced statement in Figure 11. Figures 12 and 13 were generated from the same data, but different information was requested in each column.

The user has the ability to request and print other types of custom reports. Figure 14 shows a summary report that gives information in to-

Figure 12. Computer Generated Financial Statement

Grace Baptist Church
Monthly Financial Statement
for January

| | ------ PERIOD ------ | | | ------ YTD ------ | | |
	Actual	Budget	Difference	Actual	Budget	Difference
BUDGET RECEIPTS						
Envelope Offerings	24,000.00	22,632.50	1,367.50–	24,000.00	271,590.00	247,590.00
Loose Plate Offerings	0.00	0.00	0.00	0.00	0.00	0.00
Miscellaneous Receipts	0.00	0.00	0.00	0.00	0.00	0.00
Interest	0.00	0.00	0.00	0.00	0.00	0.00
TOTAL BUDGET RECEIPTS	24,000.00	22,632.50	1,367.50–	24,000	271,590.00	247,590.00
DISBURSEMENTS						
MISSIONS MINISTRY						
Cooperative Program	2,666.66	2,666.66	0.00	2,666.66	32,000.00	29,333.34
Associational Missions	291.66	291.66	0.00	291.66	3,500.00	3,208.34
Other Missions	43.55	625.00	581.45	43.55	7,500.00	7,456.45
TOTAL MISSIONS MINISTRY	3,001.87	3,583.32	581.45	3,001.87	43,000.00	39,998.13

PASTORAL MINISTRY

Pastor Salary	1,833.33	1,833.33	0.00	1,833.33	22,000.00	20,166.67
Pastor Benefits	208.33	208.33	208.33	0.00	2,500.00	2,291.67
Housing Allowance	541.66	541.66	0.00	541.66	6,500.00	5,958.34
Car Allowance	166.66	166.66	0.00	166.66	2,000.00	1,833.34
Books and Supplies	52.00	25.00	27.00–	52.00	300.00	248.00
TOTAL PASTORAL MINISTRY	2,801.98	2,774.98	27.00–	2,801.98	33,300.00	30,498.02

CHRISTIAN EDUCATION MINISTRY

Minister of Ed. Salary	1,750.00	1,749.99	0.01–	1,750.00	21,000.00	19,250.00
Minister of Ed. Benefits	624.99	624.99	0.00	624.99	7,500.00	6,875.01
Sunday School	450.00	541.66	91.66	450.00	6,500.00	6,050.00
Church Training	95.00	125.00	30.00	95.00	1,500.00	1,405.00
WMU & Auxiliaries	325.00	375.00	50.00	325.00	4,500.00	4,175.00
Brotherhood & Auxiliaries	345.00	266.66	78.34–	345.00	3,200.00	2,855.00
Media Center	15.00	62.50	47.50	15.00	750.00	735.00
Education Supplies & Material	0.00	100.00	100.00	0.00	1,200.00	1,200.00
Other Educational Expenses	0.00	41.66	41.66	0.00	500.00	500.00
TOTAL EDUCATIONAL MINISTRY	3,604.99	3,887.46	282.47	3,604.99	46,650.00	43,045.01

Figure 13. Computer Generated Financial Statement With Layout Changed

Grace Baptist Church
Monthly Financial Statement
for January

	Budget	Month	To Date	Balance
BUDGET RECEIPTS				
Envelope Offerings	271,590.00	24,000.00	24,000.00	247,590.00
Loose Plate Offerings	0.00	0.00	0.00	0.00
Miscellaneous Receipts	0.00	0.00	0.00	0.00
Interest	0.00	0.00	0.00	0.00
TOTAL BUDGET RECEIPTS	271,590.00	24,000.00	24,000.00	247,590.00
DISBURSEMENTS				
MISSIONS MINISTRY				
Cooperative Program	32,000.00	2,666.66	2,666.66	29,333.34
Associational Missions	3,500.00	291.66	291.66	3,208.34
Other Missions	7,500.00	43.55	43.55	7,456.45
TOTAL MISSIONS MINISTRY	43,000.00	3,001.87	3,001.87	39,998.13

PASTORAL MINISTRY

Pastor Salary	22,000.00	1,833.33	20,166.67
Pastor Benefits	2,500.00	208.33	2,291.67
Housing Allowance	6,500.00	541.66	5,958.34
Car Allowance	2,000.00	166.66	1,833.34
Books and Supplies	300.00	52.00	248.00
TOTAL PASTORAL MINISTRY	33,300.00	2,801.98	30,498.02

CHRISTIAN EDUCATION MINISTRY

Minister of Ed. Salary	21,000.00	1,750.00	19,250.00
Minister of Ed. Benefits	7,500.00	624.99	6,875.01
Sunday School	6,500.00	450.00	6,050.00
Church Training	1,500.00	95.00	1,405.00
WMU & Auxiliaries	4,500.00	325.00	4,175.00
Brotherhood & Auxiliaries	3,200.00	345.00	2,855.00
Media Center	750.00	15.00	735.00
Education Supplies & Material	1,200	0.00	1,200.00
Other Educational Expenses	500.00	0.00	500.00
TOTAL EDUCATIONAL MINISTRY	46,650.00	3,604.99	43,045.01

Figure 14. Summary Financial Statement

Grace Baptist Church
Monthly Financial Statement
for January

	PERIOD			YTD		
	Actual	Budget	Difference	Actual	Budget	Difference
RECEIPTS						
Budget Receipts	24,000.00	22,632.50	1,367.50–	24,000.00	271,590.00	247,590.00
Designated Receipts	0.00	0.00	0.00	0.00	0.00	0.00
TOTAL RECEIPTS	24,000.00	22,632.50	1,367.50–	24,000	271,590.00	247,590.00
DISBURSEMENTS						
Missions Ministry	3,001.87	3,583.32	581.45	3,001.87	43,000.00	39,998.13
Pastoral Ministry	2,801.98	2,774.98	27.00–	2,801.98	33,300.00	30,498.02
Christian Education Ministry	3,604.99	3,887.46	282.47	3,604.99	46,650.00	43,045.01
Music Ministry	3,022.23	3,024.97	2.74	3,022.23	36,300.00	33,277.77
Youth & Community Ministry	465.00	429.16	35.84–	465.00	5,150.00	4,685.00
Supportive Ministry	2,446.22	3,486.64	1,040.42	2,446.22	41,840.00	39,393.78
Property and Management	12,526.58	5,529.14	6,997.44–	12,526.58	66,350.00	53,823.42
Designated Disbursements	0.00	0.00	0.00	0.00	0.00	0.00
TOTAL DISBURSEMENTS	27,868.87	22,715.67	5,153.20–	27,868.87	272,590.00	244,721.13
Excess (or deficiency) of Receipts over Disbursements	3,868.87–	83.17–	3,785.70	3,868.87–	1,000.00–	2,868.87

Figure 15. Report of Transactions for One Account

Ledger: Media Center

Jan 01,89

Name	EM.LIBR	Reconcile	
Description	Media Center	Date	000 000,00
Normal Bal	D	Balance	0.00

Next Ref#	0	Closing Bal	509.43
# of Items	4	Opening Bal	0.00

Date	Ref #	Description	Amount	Balance	Account (R)
Jan 15,89	16	Baptist Book Store – Children	15.00	165.00	BANK
Feb 06,89	32	Baptist Book Store – Comment.	295.00	460.00	BANK
Feb 09,89	33	Central Supply – Cards, Tape	12.95	472.95	BANK
Mar 09,89	34	Christian Book Store – Youth	36.48	509.43	BANK

Date	Ref #	Description	Amount	Balance	Account (R)

tals by budget category rather than in detail for each item in the budget. Figure 15 shows a detailed report of the spending to date for one specific budget account. In this special report the information given shows the individual transactions that have affected the account. Using a manual system this information would be available, but it would be time consuming to produce such reports.

Church accounting software offers many information management features for the church staff. For the person who just wants to know, "Is the money available?" the answer is easily obtained. For the administrator or pastor who becomes involved in the details of when and how money is spent, the capability exists for regular, detailed reports on the budget or specific accounts. With good accounting software, there is no reason a staff member should not be able to use the computer to look up information, produce reports, or examine accounts as desired.

In addition to information management, accounting software offers much greater accuracy and efficiency. Church requirements for financial record keeping have been increasing rapidly for years. Due to inflation and greater incomes of members, small churches may easily find themselves managing $100,000 budgets and medium-sized churches handling $500,000 or more each year. It takes a great deal of time to do the accounting for such sums. Many secretaries have found that the time needed for bookkeeping has gotten far beyond the time the church thinks is needed. **An efficient software package may be the only effective way to keep accounting under control.**

What Should You Know about Accounting?

From what you have read in this chapter you should:

• Know that a full-featured accounting software package provides the most effective method for keeping books on the computer.

• Know that good software, properly used, provides continuous, current financial information.

Note

1. Reports shown in Figures 12—14 were produced using NewViews accounting software with church model books from Church Information System, the Baptist Sunday School Board of the Southern Baptist Convention.

8

Word Processing and Desktop Publishing

Churches generate a vast amount of written materials. Sunday bulletins, newsletters, flyers, letters to members, financial statements, letters to visitors, bulletins for specials services, directories, and class rolls are just a few of the many types of written documents churches produce. If you ask a church how their computer system is helping the work of the church, most of the uses mentioned will probably involve word processing in some form. In many cases the only real use churches have found for a computer is word processing.

While word processing has tremendous benefits for churches, this should not be the primary function of the computer. If the church does not discover the possibilities of chapters 2—7 then the church has missed applications and capabilities that really make the computer a worthwhile investment. **However, churches need to make maximum use of the power of word processing and move into the area of desktop publishing as well.**

Word processing is normally thought of as the ability to handle text or words. By using a word processing software package, the operator can see typed text on the computer screen. Once the text is entered it can be modified by inserting or deleting letters, words, lines, or sections of text. Words or blocks of words can be moved. Normally the operator can have the right margin justified, place the text in columns, and check the spelling. Many more features are available, but the key is the ability to handle text or words. A document can be named and *saved* (placed in the storage system of the computer) to be retrieved and printed or further modified at a later time. *Desktop publishing*, in a technical sense, is the ability to take text from a word processor; an image, drawing, or picture from another source; or perhaps a graph from a spread sheet and create a layout on screen. Desktop publishing allows the operator to reduce or enlarge text, headlines, pictures, or illustrations and to place them. It is the ability to cut and paste a document together on a computer screen.

Advances have brought to standard word processing software many of the capabilities that have been reserved for desktop publishing software. With a word processing package like WordPerfect 5.1, the operator can insert pictures or illustrations, use enlarged text for headlines, or use a reduced type size if needed.

Dozens of books tell how to use various word processing and desktop publishing software packages. Anyone wanting advanced help with a specific software package should first go to the documentation that came with the software and then look for additional help in other books. This chapter does not attempt to do what other books have done, but it will illustrate three basic church-type applications that require the use of word processing. Two of the three applications involve using the church software in conjunction with word processing software. From this chapter you will gain a better understanding of the potential for use of word processing with emphasis on using word processing in conjunction with church software.

The Church Newsletter

A normal task for a computer in the church office is to produce a newsletter. Churches take many different approaches to newsletters. Some churches will use a weekly newsletter, while others may use a monthly newsletter. Newsletters may rely heavily on articles from staff members, while others contain only promotional material and announcements. Newsletters may include the order of service for the next Sunday and then double as the Sunday bulletin. Some typical things included in a newsletter are: pastor's article, financial and attendance figures from the previous Sunday, hospital and bereavement announcements, and a weekly or monthly calendar of activities. **Frequently those who produce the newsletter face having too little or too much material for the space available and having to deal with information that comes in late.**

The computer allows the operator to type the full newsletter on screen and then move the text around as needed. A poem included as filler might be deleted at the last minute to make room for an announcement about a men's breakfast. Layout work can be done on screen. The *pitch* (how closely the characters are spaced, usually 10, 12, or 17 characters per inch) of the type can be changed as needed to expand or contract the text. Blank lines can be deleted or added. Word processing software should be able to easily operate in column formats. The word processor will automatically justify the right margin, center headlines if needed, and type flush right for entering figures.

Once the copy is complete, the operator can use the word processor to check spelling and print the document. The newsletter can be saved to be used again the next week. The basic setup for paper size, margins, and columns should only need to be figured once. When the operator is ready to do the next week's newsletter, some things can be reused. A calendar of activities or a financial and attendance report will require editing rather than complete retyping. If staff members are also using word processing, they can bring their articles to the secretary on diskette rather than in writing, so the operator does not need to retype everything. Finished copy can be produced with a minimum of cutting and pasting before final printing or copying.

The quality of the printer determines the quality of the finished product. A program like WordPerfect 5.1 allows the operator to use almost any capability the printer has, but it still cannot do more than the printer. Today's better matrix printers produce type that is considered letter quality and looks clean, crisp, and sharp. If the print from a matrix printer is not acceptable, a laser printer becomes an option. A laser printer, because of speed, cost of operation, and limitations on types of paper and forms that can used, will not normally serve as the general purpose printer in the church office. However, for producing the best newsletters or other documents with a wide variety of type faces, type sizes, and top quality graphic images, the laser printer is the best.

A feature on the newest word processing programs is the ability to bring graphic images directly into a word processing document. This gives many churches most of the capability they need for publishing without having to use special software. Traditional clip art, frequently used by churches, is now available on diskettes. The various pictures are in files that can be retrieved and inserted at appropriate places in the newsletter.

Figures 16 and 17 illustrate possibilities for producing newsletters with word processing software. The same text is used for both Figures. Figure 16 was done with a good quality 24-pin matrix printer. The features available with WordPerfect 5.1 are indicated. Figure 17 contains the same text but was printed on a laser printer.

Figure 16. Sample Newsletter Page, Matrix Printer

Graduate Recognition

If you are a high school or college graduating senior, please send your name, photograph, degree, and plans for the future to the church office by May 17.

The Week's Activities

Sunday, April 2
  9:00 Prayer
  9:30 Library Opens
  9:45 Sunday School
 11:00 Morning Worship
  4:00 Youth Choir
  5:00 Church Training
  6:00 Evening Worship
Monday, April 3
 11:30 Baptist Women
  7:30 Deacons Meeting
Tuesday, April 4
  7:00 SS Visitation
Wednesday, April 5
  4:45 Prime Time Singers

VACATION BIBLE SCHOOL

The time has come to begin enlisting directors and workers to serve in our VBS. The date for our VBS is June 26-30.

In order to have a successful VBS, we will need your help. You have been so faithful to make our VBS a special event each summer. Through your service VBS can reach many children in the name of Christ. Through your love they can be loved. Please begin to pray about your place of service. If you have a desire to serve in a particular position call Diane Jones at 845-3298 right away.

Figure 17. Sample Newsletter Page From a Laser Printer

Graduate Recognition

If you are a high school or college graduating senior, please send your name, photograph, degree, and plans for the future to the church office by May 17.

The Week's Activities

Sunday, April 2
9:00 Prayer
9:30 Library Opens
9:45 Sunday School
11:00 Morning Worship
4:00 Youth Choir
5:00 Church Training
6:00 Evening Worship

Monday, April 3
11:30 Baptist Women
7:30 Deacons Meeting

Tuesday, April 4
7:00 SS Visitation

Wednesday, April 5
4:45 Prime Time Singers
5:45 Family Supper
6:15 Prayer Meeting
7:30 Sanctuary Choir

VACATION BIBLE SCHOOL

The time has come to begin enlisting directors and workers to serve in our VBS. The date for our VBS is June 26-30. In order to have a successful VBS, we will need your help. You have been so faithful to make our VBS a special event each summer. Through your service VBS can reach many children in the name of Christ. Through your love they can be loved. Please begin to pray about your place of service. If you have a desire to serve in a particular position call Diane Jones at 845-3298 right away.

Mailings and Mail Merge

Churches use printed materials as a means of communication. **Churches of all sizes face the problem of needing to communicate to the membership the plans, programs, and activities of the fellowship. Effective use of word processing enhances communication.** Ministers will have particular programs they want to emphasize. Encouragement to participate in programs can be done through special mailings, promotion directed at target groups, printed brochures and flyers, and regular church publications such as the Sunday bulletin and weekly newsletter.

This section examines: (1) personalized mail, (2) general mail and, (3) how both can be improved by use of target groups. Churches are one of many organizations that seek to use the mail to promote their activities. Church mail often falls into the category of junk mail that people receive every week. Word processing gives the minister the opportunity to improve the appearance of mail, personalize it, and mail it directly to target groups so that it has a better chance of being read than discarded.

Using Mail Merge for Personal Letters

Mail Merge is a feature on most word processing packages. If you are using a word processor that does not have Mail Merge or the merge feature is difficult to use, that could be a signal to investigate other packages. Mail Merge allows the operator to type a list of names and addresses as one document, type a letter as a second document, and then merge the two documents so that a personal letter is addressed to each person on the name and address list as shown in Figure 18. How this is done will vary from one word processor to another. The operator needs to type the names and addresses in the necessary format, type the letter with the correct codes to indicate where the name, address, and salutation are to be inserted, and then use the correct commands to initiate the merge.

Effective church software allows the operator to produce a merge list directly from the membership software. The names from the church software should be able to be written directly into word processing in a correct merge format. This means that preparing a letter for 20, 200, or 2000 persons only requires typing the letter one time, extracting the correct list from the church data base, and then executing the merge. Remember, there are two ways to get the merge list. One is to type the names, addresses, and salutations in word processing, and the second is to have the church software generate the merge list.

Figure 18. Merge File, Master Letter, Merged Letters

Merge File

Mr. and Mrs. Joe Banion^R
197 Springs Road
City, ST 45321^R
Joe and Ruth^R
^E
Mr. and Mrs. Jack Bowman^R
6 South Oak Dr
City, ST 45321^R
Jack and Lois^R
^E
Mr. John Cline^R
31 North Pike
City, ST 45321^R
John^R

Master Letter
Grace Baptist Church
Main and Broadway
City, ST 45321

(615) 321-5555

^F1^
^F2^

Dear ^F3^

I wanted to express my thanks to you for your willingness to serve in our Sunday School in the coming church year. The growth we have experienced has been a blessing for which we praise God. It is exciting to think about what we will see as our ministry and outreach continues. To do our best we must be trained and the best time to train is at the beginning.

Our association has a very special opportunity for each Sunday School worker to hear from the best. This year's Associational Sunday School Clinic will be on September 25 and 26 from 7 to 9 p.m. each Evening. The sessions will be divided by age group so you will be able to get the specific help you need.

Our church will host the clinic this year so we should have 100 percent partic-ipation. Reservations are not needed, just plan to be present.

Sincerely

Pastor

Merged Letters
Grace Baptist Church
Main and Broadway
City, ST 45321

(615) 321-5555

Mr. and Mrs. Joe Banion
197 Springs Road
City, ST 45321

Dear Joe and Ruth

I wanted to express my thanks to you for your willingness to serve in our Sunday School in the coming church year. The growth we have experienced has been a blessing for which we praise God.

Grace Baptist Church
Main and Broadway
City, ST 45321

(615) 321-5555

Mr. and Mrs. Jack Bowman
6 South Oak Dr
City, ST 45321

Dear Jack and Lois

I wanted to express my thanks to you for your willingness to serve in our Sunday School in the coming church year. The growth we have experienced has been a blessing for which we praise God.

Grace Baptist Church
Main and Broadway
City, ST 45321

(615) 321-5555

Mr. John Cline
31 North Pike
City, ST 45321

Dear John

I wanted to express my thanks to you for your willingness to serve in our Sunday School in the coming church year. The growth we have experienced has been a blessing for which we praise God.

What types of letters might appropriately use the merge function? How about:

- To members concerning a fund raising campaign.
- To prospective members as a personal letter from the pastor giving a welcome to the community, an invitation to a revival, or an invitation to a special service.
- To Sunday School workers emphasizing an important training event.

There are some things that should be kept in mind when preparing merge letters. Always proof the master letter carefully, and also check each merged letter. With some merge files if one field is missing, such as the address for an individual, all following letters may be done incorrectly. This might mean some letters could have an address where the salutation should be. WordPerfect protects against this type of error, but it can still occur, and in some word processing packages these mistakes are hard to prevent. Names should also be checked because it is always possible for a person's name to appear wrong. This could happen because a person had a name that they preferred for the address but a nickname that should be used for the salutation. For example a man might want the address to read "Robert," but preferred the salutation be "Dear Bob." It only takes a few minutes to page through a large number of letters on screen and visually check the addresses and salutations.

General Mail

Not all mail needs to be personalized. Many messages can be sent as flyers, invitations, or announcements. The ability of word processing to allow the operator to lay out and edit the piece on screen allows drafts to be made and easily changed. What types of documents might be sent as mass printed pieces? Consider these possibilities:

- Newsletters for choir, youth, Sunday School, singles, senior adults, and so forth,
- Announcements for special youth, children's, or recreation events,
- Revival flyers,
- Announcements for special seminars or studies.

Mail to Target Groups

A common question to ask about any material being sent from the church office is: "Who should receive this?" Computer software improves the ability to direct mailings to where they will be effective. General mail may be sent using mailing labels, and sending the material to target groups improves the results.

Target groups are selected using the church computer software. The operator selects a list of persons in the desired group and then prints mailing labels for the group or produces a merge list. This means that if the pastor wanted to send a letter to all adult women in the church, inviting them to a special seminar, it would be possible to create a selection in membership asking for:

Sex = Female
Age > 18
Church Relationship = Resident Member

Other sample target groups might be youth, parents of preschoolers, men in the church, senior adults, or persons with birthdays in June. If mailing labels are to be used they can be enhanced by adding a line of text to call attention to what might be inside, for example:

Fall Marriage Retreat
Mr. and Mrs. Tom Morris
100 Polk Place
City, ST 45321

Ladies Coffee, June 23
Mrs. Lynn Currey
321 Elm Street
City, ST 45321

It's Golf Tournament Time
Mr. James McCann
P.O. Box 254
City, ST 45321

Transferring Reports from Church Software

Reports prepared using church software can be enhanced for more effective use through word processing. For example, assume the youth workers want to call all graduating high school seniors, take reservations for a dinner hosted by the church, and find out what high school each senior is graduating from. You want to divide the youth to be called among three workers who will make the calls.

Step 1: Get the Appropriate List from the Church Software.

Church application software allows a specific list to be selected. The question of high school graduates could make selecting this list somewhat tricky. Most software packages do not list school grade as a data field. Selecting the names by age could cause a name to be overlooked if someone's birth date were missing and age may not correspond exactly with school grade. If the church had all youth enrolled in a twelfth grade Sunday School class, a list of all enrolled and prospective members might produce the proper list. The selection that would be most likely to produce all names needed would depend on the way the church had entered data, but it should be obvious that the list would need to be checked for accuracy. A minister should never assume that because the list comes from a computer it will be exactly what is desired. With the list selected, the operator would have a printout generated with the desired information, in this case the name and phone number. A sample report generated by Church Information System Touch People software is shown in Figure 21.

Step 2: Move the Report to Word Processing.

This printout would then be moved to word processing to be edited. How this moving would be accomplished would depend on how the church software program functioned. Some possibilities would be options that allowed you to: (1) export a file, (2) move a file, or (3) write a disk file.

Step 3: Edit the Layout as Needed.

Depending on the format of the report created in the church program, some editing in word processing might be required. This editing could include: creating a new page layout for left, right, top and bottom margins or deleting page headings inserted by the church software program. Further editing could be done to divide the names into groups as needed. If the intention was to divide the names among three callers then the operator could simply start a new page after each group of names as appropriate. Figure 22 shows the report broken into pages. The double lines indicate where a new page begins.

Step 4: Insert the Instructions and Headings Needed.

The report was moved to word processing to add instructions about what to do and to insert headings as needed. There are different ways of doing this in different word processing packages. Two possibilities are:

(1) Use headers and footers to insert needed extra text.

(2) Type instructions and headings on the first page and use the block and move functions to place the text on succeeding pages.

Figure 23 shows a page of a completed work sheet ready to be given to a youth worker.

The word processing applications suggested in these examples may sound difficult to someone who is new to computers. That should not worry you or stop you from using computers. Do not be concerned about sophisticated applications you have not yet had time to learn. Some pastors and staff members will never personally do the type of applications just mentioned. Knowing that such things can be done may enable you to enlist a secretary or volunteer to assist you in producing such special reports. While the work may sound complicated, it is actually routine for an experienced user.

These three applications only begin to describe what word processing can do. Each of the three can be subdivided based on doing different things. For example, the things that apply to preparing a church newsletter also apply to doing a choir, youth, single adult, or senior adult newsletter. Possibilities for merge letters apply to any type of letter that might be sent to any group selected from the church software. General documents and publicity pieces can be as creative and varied as the user de-

Figure 21. Graduating Seniors Report From Church Software

09/16/89

Grace Baptist Church
Graduating Seniors

Page: 1

Name	Phone	Yes	No	High School
Allen, Kathy	( ) 251-3488			
Anderson, Connie	( ) 251-9876			
Clements, Ronald	( ) 355-3219			
Harris, Joe	( ) 244-3454			
Jackson, Bert	(404) 234-8799			
Jones, David	( ) 251-3344			
Jones, Molly	( ) 222-4444			
Long, Richard	( ) 377-9653			
May, Steve	( ) 790-3265			
Rogers, John	( ) 233-4566			
Russou, John	( ) 234-3211			
Russell, Teresa	( ) 234-2311			
Smith, David	( ) 251-4855			
Smithe, Mona	( ) 251-8455			
Taylor, David	( ) 251-3836			
Thomas, Katie	( ) 251-4336			
Watson, Billy	( ) 222-4444			
Wilson, Sylvia	( ) 255-3465			
Wilman, Tom	( ) 255-3555			
White, Rockey	( ) 233-4709			
May, Rebecca	( ) 790-3265			
Harris, Linda	( ) 244-3454			
Deeten, Sarah	( ) 255-5671			
Dean, Karen	( ) 255-3421			
Clements, Doris	( ) 355-3219			

Figure 22. Graduating Seniors Divided Into Three Groups

09/16/89

Grace Baptist Church
Graduating Seniors

Name	Phone	Yes	No	High School
Allen, Kathy	( ) 251-3488			
Anderson, Connie	( ) 251-9876			
Clements, Ronald	( ) 355-3219			
Harris, Joe	( ) 244-3454			
Jackson, Bert	(404) 234-8799			
Jones, David	( ) 251-3344			
Jones, Molly	( ) 222-4444			
Long, Richard	( ) 377-9653			
May, Steve	( ) 790-3265			
Rogers, John	( ) 233-4566			
Russou, John	( ) 234-3211			
Russell, Teresa	( ) 234-2311			
Smith, David	( ) 251-4855			
Smithe, Mona	( ) 251-8455			
Taylor, David	( ) 251-3836			
Thomas, Katie	( ) 251-4336			
Watson, Billy	( ) 222-4444			
Wilson, Sylvia	( ) 255-3465			
Wilman, Tom	( ) 255-3555			
White, Rockey	( ) 233-4709			
May, Rebecca	( ) 790-3265			
Harris, Linda	( ) 244-3454			
Deeten, Sarah	( ) 255-5671			
Dean, Karen	( ) 255-3421			
Clements, Doris	( ) 355-3219			

Figure 23. Completed Call Sheet for Graduating Seniors

09/16/89

Page: 1

Grace Baptist Church
Graduating Seniors

Please call each senior listed below and:

1. Ask if they plan to attend the dinner for our graduates (Friday, 7:00 PM, Steak House) and check their name yes or no.

2. Ask what high school they will be graduating from and write it on this sheet.

We need your completed list by Sunday, May 5 so reservations may be made.

Name	Phone	Yes	No	High School
Allen, Kathy	251-3488			
Anderson, Connie	251-9876			
Clements, Ronald	355-3219			
Harris, Joe	244-3454			
Jackson, Bert	234-8799			
Jones, David	251-3344			
Jones, Molly	222-4444			
Long, Richard	377-9653			
May, Steve	790-3265			

sires. Word processing capabilities and the possibilities for using graphics in documents are improving constantly. If you need to put words on paper, then it can usually be done more efficiently and effectively using word processing. Churches have too great a need for communication to fail to take advantage of this aspect of computer use.

What Should You Know about Word Processing?

From the information in this chapter you should:

• Know the importance of discovering all the capabilities of a full-featured word processing package and recognize ways to put those capabilities to use in the church office.

• Realize that anything that can be done with text can be done with word processing.

9

What Else Can Be Done?

A small church in the Midwest invested a sizable amount of money in a good computer system. The church had the software to do the basic applications described in chapters 3-8. Three or four months after receiving the system, attending training, and completing installation, the pastor was still making calls, buying software, and trying to get more programs running. At one point the question was asked, "Wouldn't it be wise to stop worrying about some of these other things, and just concentrate on getting your member records entered and usable?"

Computer software of all prices and descriptions can be found anywhere from a bookstore to a toy shop. **I contend that a church needs to concentrate on learning those things that will do the most to enhance the ministry and outreach of the church.** Few would argue with such a statement, but which software produces the most work, the quickest, might be open to some disagreement. One set of guidelines that could be used to determine a priority for what software to install and operate might be:

(1) Look at the work already being done. At a minimum, you are probably maintaining member records, maintaining stewardship records, and keeping financial records.

(2) Identify those tasks that most lend themselves to computer support and that if accomplished would significantly enhance the work of the church. Members records can easily be kept on computer and open significant possibilities for ministry and communication.

(3) Install the software that will accomplish those tasks.

(4) Give the necessary time to get the software up and running, including the time to enter, check, and correct data.

(5) Move to other things that can be done with the software because the computer system is now in place and operating. If member records are being kept, it is easy to move to maintaining prospect records, Sunday School records, or records for other organizations such as choir.

(6) Once basic tasks are accomplished and being done effectively, begin to investigate other applications.

This book is designed to address the accelerated interest in computers in churches. Interest has grown because of the large number of relatively inexpensive personal computers that can be purchased today. Most churches[1] will have computers that are IBM or IBM compatible (Dell, Tandy, COMPAQ, and many more) and use the MS-DOS operating system. Some will have either Apple or Macintosh computers, and a few may use either Commodore or Atari home computers. When investigating additional software to use, read the system requirements, which will normally be found on the software package. These requirements will tell you what type of machine the software will operate on and if there are special requirements for memory, monitor, disk drives, and so forth.

There are two types of software of interest to the church. *General software* includes a wide variety of programs that could be used in a home, church, school, or business. These programs may manipulate numbers or print banners. Many are inexpensive and very useful. The second category is *application software designed especially for the church.* Application software includes programs to maintain church libraries or enhance Bible study. Bible study software will be discussed in chapter 10. This chapter is not intended to be a review of products or comparison of any products. The reader should use this information to get an idea of the broader range of computer applications available and think about what applications might prove most useful in his/her church office.

General Purpose Software

Spread Sheets

Spread sheets are computer programs originally designed to do things with numbers. A spread sheet can be visualized as a page divided into rows and columns (like a ledger sheet). Each intersection of a row and column is called a *cell.* Cells may contain numbers, formulas, or words. Formulas in cells may refer to other cells. One of the simplest uses of a spread sheet in a church is budget preparation. The example in Figure 24 shows a simplified budget preparation spread sheet. The layout is general and does not represent any specific product.

Expressions in parenthesis refer to the formulas that would be in the cells where totals are called for. Typical formulas might look like: Sum (B10:B13) or B10$^+$B11$^+$B12$^+$B13.

Figure 24. Spreadsheet for Budget Preparation

	A	B	
1			
2	Missions		
3	World	5,000	
4	Local	1,000	
5	Total Missions	6,000	(Cell B4 is the sum of B2 and B3)
6	Salaries		
7	Pastor	20,000	
8	Secretary	10,000	
9	Total Salaries	30,000	(Cell B8 is the sum of B6 and B7)
10	Ministry Support		
11	Postage	500	
12	Utilities	1,000	
13	Insurance	1,000	
14	Literature	2,500	
15	Total Support	5,000	(Cell B14 is the sum of B10, B11, B12 and B13)
	Total Budget	41,000	(Cell B15 is the sum of B4, B8, and B14)

The potential power of spread sheets is beyond what any church would normally need. Spread sheets can perform sophisticated statistical and mathematical calculations. While this type of software has far more capability than a church might use, it still has many important applications for the church. In the example above showing a simple budget, a common question would be, "What if we increase the salaries by 10 percent, how does that change the total?" If the amounts in cells B6 and B7 are increased by 10 percent all totals will also change, giving the answer to "What if?" automatically.

A spread sheet could be set up quickly so that figures like Sunday School or worship attendance could be entered each week. Calculations for average year to date or average for the month could be automatically figured. If each column represented a year, it would be possible to compare previous years at a glance. Most of the full function spread sheets will have the capability to produce graphs from the data. By using a spread sheet for entering Sunday School enrollment, church membership, and Sunday School attendance, the graph shown in Figure 25 was easily produced. Another church application for a spread sheet is to use it to tabulate and analyze results from surveys of the congregation.

Figure 25. Graph of Church Data

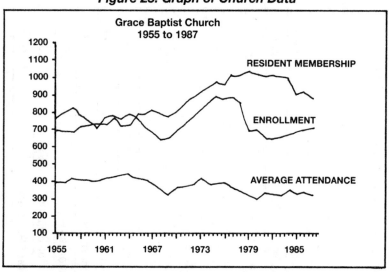

The obvious question is, "Could a spread sheet be used to do the things discussed in chapters on accounting and stewardship?" Yes, to a degree it would be possible. However, producing anything approaching the power of a full-featured accounting package would cost more in time than the results would ever produce in work. Keeping stewardship information by person, fund, and Sunday and having the ability to generate quarterly statements would be a practical impossibility in the average church situation.

A key factor in using spread sheets is that they are essentially do it yourself. The user must expect to buy the software and then learn to operate it by reading the manual and documentation with the software. Good documentation will offer simple lessons that can be easily followed. For a person with some computer background, spread sheets are not difficult, but they must be learned, and the user must figure out applications.

Graphics

The term *graphics* can refer to many different things in computer software. Examples are:
- the ability of spread sheets to produce graphs,
- inserting pictures or clip art into text in word processing,
- software that will produce charts or transparencies,
- illustrations or pictures used in desktop publishing,
- software that will easily produce simple signs, banners, and invitations.

It should also be noted that there is a major technical difference between text and graphics. In this sense, text is letters, numbers, and special characters produced by pressing a key on the keyboard (a, b, 1, $, •, "). Graphics are images on screen produced by the actual dots that make up a screen image.

Quite a selection of relatively inexpensive graphic packages is available. These low-cost products offer significant help to churches. Anyone can see the results of this software daily. Schools, hospitals, and even displays in flea markets will routinely have signs that are produced by a computer. Many times these signs and banners will have come from low-cost, easy-to-operate graphic packages. Such software may sell for around $50. The lower cost versions will be limited in what they produce. A sign might only be able to be printed in an 8½- by 11-inch format. The number of possible lines of lettering and number of characters per line may also be fixed. The quality of output will be directly related to the printer being used. Within these limits, and with a little imagination, the operator can probably do quite a number of useful things. Software of this nature is readily available in computer shops, bookstores, and department stores.

Other General Purpose Software

A few minutes browsing in a computer shop or store with a wide selection of off-the-shelf software will acquaint the reader with a wide variety of software. Cost will be a factor in what may be tried. Stores do not normally accept a return on software. Stores will probably not allow you to take a package home, remove the wrapping, load and use the software, and then decide to return it. More and more you are being held responsible for reading the requirements and being sure the software you purchase will run on your equipment. Purchasing decisions for off-the-shelf software will often be made on friend's recommendations, magazine reviews, or descriptions on the package.

Some of the types of software you that might interest you could include any of the following:

● *Label/Badge Making.* These packages produce a wide variety of labels. These are not mailing labels. The labels produced might be badges that conference participants are given to wear or labels to be put on books, folders, and so forth. The labels might be stick on or fit plastic pin-on holders.

● *Certificate Making.* You can purchase software to produce a variety of special certificates. These might be for attendance, appreciation, recognition, or anything else. The software gives the capability, and the operator supplies the idea and design.

● *Calendars.* Many of the low-cost graphics packages include the ability to print monthly or weekly calendars. Other packages are for appointment calendars and can be set to beep when it is time for you to go to a meeting. Since "this software produces a calendar" has a wide range of meanings, a user wanting this function would be advised to know what was desired and study the software carefully.

● *Filing.* A wide range of filing programs exist. These may be called notebooks, file systems, or may even use the term data base. Low cost packages (under $100) will not be powerful, sophisticated data bases but may suit the user's needs. Understanding what a filing program does may be like imagining an electronic 3- by 5-inch card system. The program allows you to determine what goes on the card. It is possible to do some of the functions discussed under membership using some simple filing programs. Limitations will occur in amount of data that can be kept, degree of integration, and other such functions. Some filing programs are for specific applications such as a program to maintain and label videotapes.

New applications and new solutions for old applications are constantly appearing. It is not a wise investment of money to purchase a lot of software that is never used, but at the same time, some small expenditures can buy some useful and good software. The user must look at what can be done and make some decisions.

Other Church Application Software

Media Library

Many churches have sizable libraries that are frequently used by members. **Maintaining a library of several thousand volumes including books, filmstrips, audio cassettes, and videocassettes is a significant task. It is also a task that is well suited to the computer.** The user needs to maintain several pieces of data for each title in the library. This includes title, author, call number, publisher, copyright date, and type of media. Other items such as accession number and number of copies might also be desired.

The operator needs to know whether the book is in the library, checked out, or being repaired. If the book is out, a record must be kept of who has it and when it is due. This type of data management lends itself very well to a computer. Media Library software is available at reasonable prices and from the same vendors who provide church management packages.

The staff member looking at putting media library software to use, should consider several things. Assume a church has a computer system in the church office. If the media library is to be supported by computer how will it be done? Will the librarian go to the church office to do his or her work? Will the church purchase a separate system and have it in the library strictly for a library system? Can a terminal in the library be connected to the main system?

In many cases the best solution will be to have a separate unit in the library. The question of cost will be raised. One way to look at cost is to consider the church's investment in its library. The books in even a small library could easily be worth $35,000, and a large library could be worth over $150,000. Furthermore, in most churches a volunteer staff will catalog and circulate the media. Volunteer time is a critical resource. If a volunteer is available and willing to put a computer to effective use, then an investment of a few thousand dollars in a system for the library could prove very wise. Skillfully operated, the computer would make the library more accessible and usable for the congregation and at the same time, protect the church's investment by providing better control over the media.

Ordering Church Literature

As of this writing, at least one major denomination is making software available to churches to assist them in ordering literature. In 1986 the Sunday School Board of the Southern Baptist Convention began giving churches software that would prepare their church literature order. The software has improved significantly since that time. One of the interesting aspects of this software, called the Electronic Order System, is that it gives the church the option of sending its order directly to the Sunday School Board via telephone modem. A *modem* is a device that attaches to a computer and allows the computer to send data over a regular telephone line.

Possibilities for software applications are endless. Many more software programs will be developed in years to come. The user should concentrate on getting work done rather than acquiring new software. **Effective use of a few good software programs produces tremendous results, while having many programs that are never used produces nothing.**

What Should You Know about
What Else Can Be Done?

From the information in this chapter you should:

● Know the importance of mastering the software you have before investing money in additional programs.

● Be able to list at least five types of software packages available for use in the church office.

Note

1. One survey has indicated that 86 percent of the computers in churches are either IBM or IBM compatible.

10

Just for the Minister

One important means of helping the ministry of the church is to help church leaders become more efficient. This chapter examines ways computers can help any minister or church staff member do his or her work better. The previous chapters have suggested numerous computer applications. These applications include many creative ways to put information about members and prospects to use to reach out to people and to minister to personal needs. Hopefully, by this point you have begun thinking of other ways to use the power of computers in your work.

In the process of performing ministry, there is much the minister must do. Daily work includes preparing sermons, devotionals, and studies; writing numerous letters and articles; maintaining personal files and libraries; and planning for both present and future events. The minister who can rely on completely adequate and effective secretarial help is most fortunate. Like other organizations, budgets alone prohibit most churches from hiring all of the secretarial help that could be used. Because of lack of help, often many things just aren't done or are not done in the way they should be.

In addition to administrative support, a minister who masters the use of a personal computer can solve the problem of lack of clerical assistance. This may be a bold claim, but it is true. However, before a computer can become the minister's personal secretary, the minister must master key applications like word processing and the operating system. Furthermore, it may be necessary to learn to do some things in a different manner to use the computer most effectively as a resource.

Word Processing

Word processing will be the biggest single use of the computer for most ministers. The advantages in using word processing justify taking the time to go to class to learn to type. Word processing is the area where people who decide to use the computer may need to change their way of getting things done. Let us discuss three different approaches.

Minister 1 has always typed. He owns a good electric typewriter and uses it constantly. He types sermon outlines and any other materials needed. In the absence of a secretary, he does his own letters. If he had a secretary, he would type a draft of the letter and give it to her to type a clean copy for his signature.

Minister 2 prefers a sharp pencil and legal pad. He makes notes and roughs out ideas. When a secretary is available, he will have appropriate materials typed. When a secretary is not available, he will type those things that absolutely must be typed such as business correspondence.

Minister 3 has learned to use a cassette recorder effectively. He does sermon outlines and letters on the recorder. His secretary transcribes the material. He also uses the cassette to play back sermon thoughts and work out his sermon with a pencil and paper.

Is typing essential to using a computer for word processing? Actually, no it is not. I know one person who came to be quite proficient at the two-finger, hunt-and-peck method. However, I would contend that the individual who knows even the least basics of touch typing will find the computer ideal for his needs. Any of the three ministers could begin with word processing, if they wanted to start using a computer. The basic change for all three is that they work, not on the typewriter, legal pad, or cassette, but at the keyboard. The secret to using the computer as your personal secretary is to transfer as much of the work to the machine at the earliest possible stage.

Assume that the minister is preparing a sermon. Instead of reaching for paper and pencil, he turns on the computer and uses the word processing program. He begins typing. He may type a title, scripture reference, and then quit. Quitting will mean giving the document a name and saving it as a file. In some systems the document will be named when the process is begun and in others it will be named when the session is over.

The minister returns to the task later. He retrieves the file. At this point, he may reword the title and put in an outline consisting of the points of the sermon. The outline may be expanded to include sub-points and illustrations. Again, when the work is done it is saved. A few days later, having thought about the message further, he again retrieves the document and adds a full section in the middle, moves an illustration at the beginning to the closing of the message, and then re-reads the outline from start to finish. At this point, it is ready and can be printed to be delivered. If the minister preaches from a manuscript rather than an outline, the process remains the same.

The key point is that the writing is done on the computer. **The ability to revise and correct makes word processing so valuable.** The hands are on the keyboard, and the eyes are on the screen. The aim is not speed; the aim is putting your thoughts and ideas on screen, well written and clearly expressed. Some things, like an important letter to the congregation on a new building project, may be carefully read to be sure each phrase is just right. Corrections and changes are simple.

Word processing does much more than just allow text to be corrected and moved on screen. Good packages will allow spelling to be checked and corrected. They have a thesaurus available to improve word usage. Documents may be changed from 10 pitch (Pica) to 12 pitch (Elite) or to condensed sizes like 15, 17, or 20 pitch. Line spacing (single or double) can be changed and right margins automatically justified. Text can be placed in columns or underlined; words or sentences can be done in bold face; and centering is done automatically. Top quality products like WordPerfect are easy to use for basic work and have sophisticated applications that are available as the operator begins to discover other needs.

Operating System (DOS)

A pastor ordered a system for his church. He intended to buy two computers. One would be a large unit to be placed in the church office for membership, stewardship, accounting, and other church work. In addition, he would have a smaller unit in his office. He asked how he could leave instructions for his secretary or do work on his machine that he could give to her. Many ministers already have or plan to have machines at home and will need to bring work from home to the office. These questions raise the issue of knowing something about the operating system.

If the minister is going to operate a personal computer effectively, he or she must understand some basics about the operating system. *DOS* stands for Disk Operating System. DOS is software that functions when the system is turned on. When the computer is turned on DOS automatically loads. This brings the computer to a point where it is ready to take commands or operate programs. The user should have a DOS manual supplied when the machine was purchased. Book stores sell many different books on using DOS. Many are hard to read. An hour or two with a friend who knows the system may be a good alternative.

How much do you need to know about the operating system? Remember, there are different operating systems for different computers. The three systems most likely to be encountered are IBM or IBM compatible, all of which use MS-DOS or PC-DOS, Apple or Macintosh, and Commodore. Some basic procedures are listed below. This section is not intended to be an instruction manual but a guideline for what needs to be learned from a manual or a friend.

(1) How to format a diskette.

(2) How to read the directory of a floppy or hard disk.

(3) How to switch between different disk drives or operate between floppy drives and hard disks.

(4) How to copy a file from one disk to another or from a hard drive to a floppy disk.

(5) How to install programs on a disk drive.

(6) How to make a backup.

This may sound a little overly technical. It isn't really. Understanding basics about the operating system will help you understand much more clearly how the system functions and make most software packages easier to learn.

Bible Study Software

The possibility of using the computer to enhance Bible study will have great appeal to most ministers. Bible study software has been available for several years but has improved greatly and declined in price. The key function is access to the Bible text. A particular program will be purchased in one of the various translations. The program will enable the operator to do word searches, find the number of occurrences of a word, view the chapter and verse references, and print portions of Scripture.

An illustration of the use of such software may be helpful. A Sunday School lesson was being prepared on the subject of God's promises. Using EveryWord Bible, a search of the *New International Version* text revealed sixty-five verses where the word *promise* was used. Each verse was scanned using the software to locate verses that referred to God's promises or gave some insight into the nature of God's promises. Verses that fell into this category were marked to be printed. Eight verses were selected using this procedure. These verses were printed as a handout for the Sunday School class. The completed handout is shown in Figure 26. It took less than five minutes to produce the handout, including searching for the verses, scanning them and marking them, and making the printout. Marking and printing the verses involved creating a file and transferring the file to word processing. The procedure is simple but does require the basic knowledge of DOS already discussed.

Figure 26. Bible Study Handout

Psalm 77:8
Has his unfailing love vanished forever? Has his promise failed for all time?

Psalm 119:41
May your unfailing love come to me, O Lord, your salvation according to your promise;

Psalm 119:50
My comfort in my suffering is this: Your promise preserves my life.

Psalm 119:58
I have sought your face with all my heart; be gracious to me according to your promise.

Psalm 119:76
May your unfailing love be my comfort, according to your promise to your servant.

Psalm 119:116
Sustain me according to your promise, and I will live; do not let my hopes be dashed.

Psalm 119:154
Defend my cause and redeem me; preserve my life according to your promise.

Psalm 119:170
May my supplication come before you; deliver me according to your promise.

This is one possible application for Bible study software. Text can be marked and moved into a sermon, article, or church newsletter. Searches can also be done on combinations of words such as love and war, mercy and grace, or Jesus and love. One question the minister will face in selecting and using a Bible program is deciding on translation. In different translations different words may be used. A search for the word love in the *New International Version* of the Bible will reveal 508 verses using the word love while the same search of the *King James Version* text will produce 280 verses.

Some ministers will be interested in software that also incorporates Greek and Hebrew texts. These types of packages are available also.

Filing with a Personal Computer

Ministers have significant needs in the area of filing. The statement is obvious but the solutions are not. **Many ministers and church staff members have resorted to filing by stack. Stacks of material are placed on the desk, floor, bookshelf, and credenza. The computer may not be the answer to all filing needs, but it can certainly help.** One point that should be made is that if you cannot maintain some sort of reasonable filing system without a computer, then you probably cannot keep a file with one. The basic point of a filing system is to retrieve information. When thinking about setting up a file, ask yourself, "What information needs to be retrieved and why?

Minister's Personal Library

Ministers assemble and use a personal library. Do the materials need to be filed? A personal library might be filed for any of the following reasons:

(1) To keep an accurate inventory of books.

(2) To keep track of who has borrowed items so that they can be recovered if not returned.

(3) To allow searches of books by author, title, or subject.

Software designed to keep a large media library could be more than many ministers want. Simpler programs are available to maintain personal libraries.

Sermons

A pastor could easily prepare over 150 sermons and Bible studies in a year. Over a period of five, ten, or twenty years and beyond, the volume of material increases to significant proportions. A minister could want to know how many messages had been preached from a given book, passage, or particular subject. He might want to know what message was preached on a certain date or for the past three Easters. Computers can assist in filing and selecting sermons. Sermons are prepared in a word processing package.

A number of notebook or data base programs exist that a minister might use to set up a sermon file. With a program like WordPerfect Library a file could be set up to keep the following:

Date Sermon Preached:
Sermon Title:
Book: Chapter: Verses:
Subject:
Related Subjects:
Place Preached:

The sermon filing system requires that once a week or once a month, the minister enters any new sermons into the data base. The information for each sermon would become a record for that sermon. The program, such as WordPerfect Library, allows searching the file of sermon records for a particular date, range of dates, or specific Bible reference.

These four applications do not cover all that might be done with a computer. It is not unusual to have someone ask, "Is there software for writing a book or dissertation." The answer is, "Yes, any good full-featured word processor will do the work you want to do."

The secret to computers is to get started, try things, and decide that you will learn to use the machine. You will not start to understand what can be done until you begin putting the computer to use.

What Should You Know about
Software for Ministers?

From what you have read in this chapter you should:

• Realize the importance of being comfortable working with certain types of software, especially word processing software.

• Know how spread sheets can help you in ministry.

• Be able to list three types of software that could be helpful in your ministry.

• Recognize possible uses for Bible study software packages.

11

Some Words on Hardware

By now, you may have questions about computer hardware. A simple test will let you know whether this chapter will tell you anything you do not already know. Consider the three advertisements below. All three came from the computer section of a retail catalog. Can you read the ads and have some idea why one computer was priced differently from the others and why you might choose one over the other? Comments about hardware refer to IBM or IBM compatible computers. Most of the hardware terms would be the same for Apple, Atari, or Commodore machines, but the chapter is written with IBM-type equipment in mind.

Computer 1:   AT/286 Compatible 3-speed computer. 64OK RAM, 1 3½" 1.44 Mb and 1 20 Mb drive, 6, 8, & 12 MHz speeds, 1 parallel, 1 serial, & 1 mouse port, 3 16-bit expansion slots, slot for Intel 80287l0NTL math chip. DOS 3.3 and GW BASIC, EGA, CGA, MGA and composite video compatible. $1,494.96.

Computer 2:   Dual Speed 20 Mb Hard Drive Computer. Features 640K RAM, 8088 microprocessor operating at 4.77 and 10 MHz, 3 expansion slots, single 5.25" 360 Kb and a 20 Mb drive, 8087lNTL math chip slot, serial and parallel ports. Includes MS DOS 3.3, PFS First Choice, and diagnostics software. Offers full IBM PC/XT compatibility. Provides MGA video and also supports CGA color. $1,098.84

Computer 3:   Dual Drive Computer System. 640K RAM, two 5.25" floppy drives, 2 speeds—4.77/10 MHz. CGA (color) and MGA (mono) video.

Serial and parallel ports, clock/calendar. Includes MS DOS 3.3, GW BASIC, and word
processing software. Phoenix Bios, and 3 open
slots. 1 year limited warranty. $696.92

As you read these three ads did you recognize the following: hard drive versus dual floppy drives and 80286 (AT) versus 8088 (XT) microprocessor (CPU)?

If you noticed these differences, you probably will find little if anything new in this chapter, but it will still be a good review for you. If neither the ads or the above distinctions mean anything to you then the chapter is designed to help. There is also a glossary of terms in the back of the book. We will begin with the basic types of computers and then talk more specifically about personal computers.

Main Frame Computers

Large businesses, colleges and universities, and government agencies will have main frame computers. These devices are large in size and located in special rooms. Terminals are connected to them either by phone line or cable. A terminal consists of a screen and keyboard. Software for main frames is probably custom designed for the particular application. The institution or organization probably has a section, unit, or department of analysts and programmers who operate the system. Costs for main frame systems range from hundreds of thousands to the millions of dollars plus the costs for the programmers.

Mini-Computers

Mini-computers are found in some churches, doctors offices, pharmacies, auto parts stores, and many other small operations. They are physically small enough not to require a special room. They may be the size of a file cabinet or even small enough to sit on a desk. The cost for a mini will be $25,000 to $100,000. Mini-computers allow terminals to be attached. The number of terminals may range from four to twenty or more. Additional terminals do increase cost. Software will be limited. Typical mini users will buy a system with software to do a specific job.

Personal Computers (PCs)

Obviously, main frames and mini-computers are too expensive for the average church. The personal computers began a revolution in computer use. By the mid-1980s it was possible to buy personal computer systems (hardware only and without a hard drive) for under $2,000. Churches invest $3,500 to $9,000 to install a single-unit personal computer system depending on computer, software, printer, monitor and other related considerations.

The personal computer was designed to be a *personal* computer. This means it was designed to be a single-user system. The operating system of the computer was written to allow one operator to work on one program doing one task at one time. One of the most common questions to be asked is, "Can I attach another screen and keyboard to my PC?" The answer is, "No, but . . . ." There are always exceptions and alternatives. Before considering exceptions, we will first look at the personal computer as it was designed to be—a personal computer.

If you look at a PC in a magazine in a store, you generally see three parts, a screen or monitor, keyboard, and box which is the computer itself. Something (a microprocessor or CPU) inside the box can process data. The keyboard allows you to send commands, data, or information to the CPU so work can be done. Differences exist in keyboards. The standard at this time is a 101-key enhanced keyboard. This gives the operator a standard typewriter layout with additional computer keys such as Alternate (ALT) and Control (CTRL), plus three other sets of keys: one for numbers, one for cursor controls, and twelve function keys. Less expensive machines may not have separate key pads. The monitor allows you to see what you are entering or see what work is occurring. If you are typing a letter, you see the words appear on the monitor. To make corrections, use the keyboard to type them, and corrections occur on screen. The main components of a PC system will be discussed individually.

Computer (PC) Processors

The CPU is the part that actually does the computing. Computers 1 and 2 in the ads sound similar, but one is $400 more than the other. The difference in price is caused by the CPU used. IBM or IBM compatible PCs first used the 8088 microprocessor. Later models used the 8086 processor. Then the IBM AT and its compatibles used the 80286 processor. There is little difference between the 8088 and 8086 CPUs, but the introduction of 80286 chip created a significant improvement in speed and power. In 1987 machines came into the market using the 80386 processor, and in 1989 80486 CPUs were introduced. To illustrate the advance with the 80386 CPU, this processor can act and function like multiple 8088 processors with each doing different tasks.

For personal (home) use, in word processing only, or maintaining a small number of records in a simple data base, a computer with the 8088 or 8086 processor would be sufficient. For accounting uses or the majority of church applications (as opposed to home/personal use) the 80286 processor should be considered a minimum. When considering the possibilities of the 80386 processor, and in some cases the 80286 CPUs, other considerations arise. The PC is a personal computer designed for one operator to work on one machine to do one task at one time. However, since PCs have been in offices, users have wanted the capabilities of mini-computers at the price and simplicity of personal computers. Churches want to put keyboards on all desks and have multiuser capabilities. There are ways this can be done, but there are no ways it can be done inexpensively or simply. The power of the 80386 processor has made it possible for churches to look to multiuser solutions with PCs in a price range of $13,000 to $25,000 for three or four users[1] on a system. Such a system can rival the performance of a comparable mini-computer costing much more. It is beyond the scope of this book to discuss these options but they include:

• Networking software like Novell that ties individual PCs together and works off of a host called a file server.

• Multiuser Operating systems like Unix or SCO-Xenix that can run on 80286 processors but have really become viable on 80386 machines.

• A number of other approaches that use large amounts of memory on 80386 machines to allow the CPU to do multiple functions.

Storage Devices or Disk Drives

Whatever work is done, you will want to be able to save the work for later use. In the case of a church, you will want to save the names, addresses, and much more information about members and prospects. Saving or storing data requires some type of device to do the storage. The first PCs stored data on cassette tapes. This worked but limited the amount of data that could be stored and the speed of reading it. Personal computers did not become practical for commercial use until better storage devices were developed.

Storage units fall into two categories: floppy drives and hard or fixed drives. Many readers have a PC that has one or two *floppy drives.* These storage units allow data, information, and programs to be kept on either a 5.25- or 3.5-inch diskette. The user is still limited by the amount of data that can be kept on an individual diskette. Some programs such as an electronic concordance of the Bible may not work on a floppy drive system. *Hard drives* are units that are inside the computer. They are storage devices that allow large amounts of data or programs to be stored and accessed. The size of a storage device is measured in terms of *bytes*. One byte is the basic unit of memory a computer recognizes. One byte can represent one character of text for instance: a, A, 1, 9, ?, /, >, or a space. The capacity in bytes is given in terms of K (Kilo, approximately $1,000^2$), or M (Mega or approximately 1,000,000). How this works in terms of the devices discussed and the three ads used is shown in Figure 27.

Figure 27. Storage Units in Increasing Size

Floppy Drives	Approximate Storage Capacity
360 KB 5.25"	360,000 Bytes on a 5.25 inch diskette
720 KB 3.5"	720,000 Bytes on a 3.5 inch diskette
1.2 MB 5.25	1,200,000 Bytes on a 5.25 inch diskette
1.44 MB 3.5	1,440,000 Bytes on a 3.5 inch diskette

Hard or Fixed Drives
20 MB   20,000,000 Bytes on the hard drive.
Hard drives are available in various sizes including, 20, 30, 40, 44, 60, 70, 90, 100, 110, 150 and 322 MB.

The absolute minimum a computer would have to have to operate would be one floppy drive. A typical system today would be a machine with one floppy drive and a hard drive. A computer with a hard drive must have one floppy drive as well. The floppy drive serves at least two purposes. When software is purchased, the programs come on diskette. The user *loads* (installs) the program onto a computer with a hard drive by inserting the diskette with the program into the floppy drive and *copying* (transferring) the program from the floppy drive to the hard drive of the unit. The second major purpose is to make *backups* of data. Backups make a duplicate copy of data or programs on a floppy disk in case the hard disk is damaged or fails to operate properly.

If you are considering purchasing a computer for home or personal use, you should buy a system with a hard drive. It is worth the extra cost of a few hundred dollars. A church should not consider using a machine without a hard drive unless it might serve as a terminal or work station on a multiuser system. Having given this advice there still may be exceptions and valid reasons for using a dual floppy machine, but the user should know and understand the limitations.

Computer Memory

At this point another component needs to be introduced which is confusing to many persons. We have discussed storage in terms of diskettes and the amount of data that can be placed on a floppy or hard disk. The new component is Random Access Memory (RAM) and is often confused with storage but is actually a different concept. *RAM* is the working memory of the computer. When a computer is turned on, a certain amount of data or programs can be brought into the machine's memory to be worked with. When the computer is turned off the programs are lost because the Random Access Memory functions only when the power is on. RAM works in conjunction with the storage device, whether it is a hard drive or floppy drive. Programs are kept either on floppy drives or the hard drive. When the computer is on, the operator brings up or loads into RAM the desired program from the drive and works with it. When the work is finished the program is saved, the operator exits the program, and turns off the machine.

An example may illustrate the concept. A pastor turns on a computer, brings up word processing, and writes a sermon. The program was on a hard disk or floppy disk, but the work has been done in RAM or in the random memory of the computer. At this point the new sermon is in the random memory. If the pastor simply turns off the machine the sermon is lost. He must save the sermon on a floppy or hard disk, then exit the program and turn off the machine. Different software programs may have different requirements for the amount of RAM needed to allow the program to operate. RAM, like storage, is measured in bytes and also in terms of either K (kilo) or M (mega). A typical PC will have at least 640 KB or 640,000 bytes of RAM. Older PCs may only have 256 KB or perhaps 512 KB of RAM.

A Quick Comparison

Now that we have discussed CPUs, hard disks, and RAM it is possible to better illustrate what has occurred in recent years. In 1981 a lower cost mini-computer with 128 KB RAM and a 15 MB hard drive sold for about $20,000. If you read the three ads that began this chapter you will see a PC with 640 KB RAM and a 20 MB hard drive for $1,098.94.

Monitors

A standard monitor for a PC originally was a monochrome monitor. The text on the screen was either amber or green in color. Color monitors were available but were much lower in resolution, which means they looked fuzzy. Today, the resolution of color monitors has increased significantly, and they are more and more widely used. PC software quickly began to demand the capabilities to display not only text (keyboard characters, letters, numbers, and symbols) but also graphics (pictures, maps, graphs, and charts). PCs may or may not have the capability built in to send signals to monitors to display color and/or graphics.

These various capacities for using color and for using graphics are specified by terms like: CGA—Color Graphics Adapter, EGA—Enhanced Graphics Adapter, and VGA—Video Graphics Adapter (which may be color or monochrome). If a PC did not have the required capability and the operator wanted that ability, an adapter card could normally be added to allow the desired use. Sometimes low-cost PCs require a card that may cost $300 or more to have graphic capabilities on screen. VGA is the current standard for monitors.

Ads for PCs may or may not include the monitor in the price. When shopping and comparing you must be sure that the monitor, CPU, storage capacity, RAM, and other options are comparable before the price of one computer can truly be compared to another.

Printers

Like everything else related to computers, printers vary widely in terms of price and capabilities. Printers range from $200 to $4000. No single printer on the market today will do everything a church might want to do. There are two basic printers in use with distinctly different functions. One is a matrix printer and the other is a laser printer.

Matrix printers use a series of wires or pins to strike a ribbon and create a character. Two types of matrix printers are sold, one using a 9-pin print head and one using a 24-pin print head. The 24-pin printer forms letters that look much more like typed characters. Prices for matrix printers vary depending on the print head, carriage width, speed, and quality of print. The printer may or may not come with a tractor feed or other device to pull continuous feed forms through the printer. Better quality printers have attachments available to feed cut-sheet paper or letterhead stationery into the printer. A church office should have a matrix printer as a part of the system. High quality matrix printers can do what most churches need done. They can produce church bulletins, newsletters, and correspondence. Because they can also print in high speed modes at less than true letter quality, they are ideal for mailing labels, attendance cards and checklists, stewardship statements, and routine reports and lists.

However, churches are finding that the quality of matrix printers doesn't quite measure up in all cases. Many churches want to produce copy that has a typeset look. This copy might be for the newsletter and bulletin or for invitations, handbills, advertising pieces, and other special items. Given the cost of typesetting, many churches can afford to invest in a higher resolution printer, if the cost is right. This need is met by the laser printer. Laser printers produce high resolution copy. They allow a wide range of fonts and type sizes. Laser printers are slower and more expensive. Prices start at about $1,500. Laser printers are not cost effective for many printing needs, and the kinds of paper that they will print on are limited. In spite of these limitations, the quality of copy from a laser makes it useful and possibly a money-saving device in many offices.

MS-DOS/PC-DOS Operating Systems

The operating system for a computer is a piece of software; however, since it is integral to any operation of the equipment, it is often considered with the hardware. It is possible to own and/or operate a computer without ever understanding or being able to work directly with the operating system. Multiuser operating systems, whether designed for minicomputers or for the more powerful PCs, are extremely complex. MS-DOS, or the IBM version PC-DOS, is not overly complex, at least for routine tasks, and is easily mastered by most users.

If you use a computer and do not understand the operating system, you will rely on someone else to do such things as install new software, delete old software, transfer programs and files from one machine to another, do backups, and perform other similar functions. Someone in the church office will almost certainly need to have some knowledge of basic operating system tasks.

Computers and Software Licenses

Churches deal with copyright laws, especially in the area of music. Computer software is protected by copyright and is sold with a specific software license. The normal license does not allow you to purchase a piece of software and install it on several different computers. A typical license is given below.

License Statement

This software is licensed for the exclusive use of the original purchaser on one computer only.

This software is not copy protected. You may make backup copies of the software for your archives only for the sole purpose of protecting your investment from loss.

You are free to move this software from one computer location to another, as long as there is no possibility of it being used at one location while it is being used at another. Just like a book cannot be read by two different people at two different locations at the same time, neither can this software be used by two different people at the same time without being in violation of the license and copyright.

Churches should understand and respect the license agreement. Be sure you read the agreement for the software you are using. Some types of software may allow you to purchase site licenses to allow other users. Multiuser software may be sold for a specific number of users or for an unlimited number of work stations using the software.

What Should You Know about Hardware?

From what you have read in this chapter you should:

● Know the basic components of a system including computer, keyboard, monitor, and printer.

● Be aware of significant differences in systems based on which CPU is used and how much memory and disk size is offered.

● Be aware of the need to be sure equivalent systems are compared in looking at price.

● Know that PCs are single user and that using PCs in multiuser operations is neither simple nor inexpensive, but there are effective ways of setting up multiuser PC systems.

● Have some idea of the difference between matrix and laser printers.

● Understand license agreements.

Notes

1. Prices and numbers of users for multiuser systems are general terms. New developments are occurring and hardware prices are changing.

2. K is not a metric term. Kilo (small k) in metric is 1,000. One K or Kb (Kilobytes) in computer terms is 1024 which is the tenth power of two. M or Mb (Megabytes) is really 1000 K or 1,024,000. Thinking of these in terms of thousands and millions is close enough for understanding.

12

Final Thoughts: Three Questions with Answers

Question 1

Okay, I've read the book, but what do I really need to know about computers? The first response to answer such a question is another question. What is your job and what do you want to do with a computer? Five different situations will be considered all in light of getting maximum use from what is available.

Situation 1

As pastor, you are the only staff member. You want a computer to help you get more done and be more effective. You want to use the computer to help make up for the secretary and staff you do not have.

First, you will have to move toward a fair degree of computer literacy. There are people in practically any church today who work with or know computers and can help you, but they will not be available every time you need them. With a good printer and basic software, the computer can be a tremendous asset. You must know the operating system well enough to do basic tasks such as installing new software or loading software updates. You must also learn to operate the software. This would normally include word processing, a membership package, and perhaps a Bible module.

Possibly a volunteer person or small committee of computer literate persons could help you put the membership list on the machine and perhaps keep it updated. Once the basic records are added, it probably will not be too difficult to make routine additions, deletions, and address changes. Whether these will be done by you or by a volunteer will depend on the situation, but no more than an hour a week should be needed to keep the records updated, unless there were an unusually large number of additions at one time or perhaps a large number of prospects to be added from a survey. In the single staff situation, a computer gives the pastor the ability to do things effectively that could never be done otherwise, but the price for the capability is the price of learning the system.

Situation 2

You are pastor of a church with several staff members. Your church has a sizable investment in a computer system, but you really want to know as little as possible about it.

You do not plan to operate the system at all. You need to know what the system can and cannot do for you. You must understand that the computer is a machine and is not unlimited in how it can output information. If you want the computer to support a plan for having the staff visit all church members over a period of weeks or months, you will have to work within the bounds of what your software can produce. The more you understand, the less likely you are to have someone tell you a particular job could not be done, when in fact, there was a way.

Situation 3

You are the pastor of a church with several staff members, but you want to understand your system fully, know what it can do, and know where you can put it to personal use.

This situation is not unlike the single staff pastor. The biggest difference is that you are, or should be, assured of competent, regular secretarial help to enter records and keep the system updated. You should learn to use word processing and use it to the point of competency. You should find out how to extract information from your church software and what options and formats are available for printing reports. This is the point at which secretaries are often weak even if they are competent in entry and updating records. In this situation you probably should not have to be concerned about learning the operating system. If you find you are the expert, having to know the operating system and all software, and everyone depends on your knowledge, you may have some secretaries or staff members that are not learning all they should. You will not learn too much or more than you should but others should be learning as well.

Situation 4

You are a staff member in a church with a computer system. You do not want to learn to operate the system or use it directly.

It should be said that in the future staff members will be expected to have some degree of computer literacy. At least you should be able to ask someone, presumably a secretary, to give you information or reports that enable you to use the system to support your particular ministry. A minister of music or recreation should as a minimum be keeping choir enrollment or recreation enrollment on the system. It would be most inefficient to have a $5,000 or $25,000 computer system with all member's names, addresses, and phone numbers but require a secretary to keep a separate manually, maintained mailing list for a particular ministry.

Situation 5

You are a staff member and want to have the full ability to use the computer system to its best advantage.

In this situation you need to learn the operating system (at the user level) and full operation of software that applies to your ministry. It can be said that in churches where computers are being effectively used, either the pastor or a staff member, has learned the system and sees that it is used. The staff member should not become the secretary, but he or she should know the system well enough to do the work and to train a secretary. Getting full use of the system means doing things like adding a spread sheet package and finding out how that software could be used to analyze and study church trends. This is certainly a much more sophisticated level of application. As churches seek staff members in the next five to ten years they will look and perhaps begin to require this type of expertise.

None of these situations (1, 3, and 5) that required a high degree of expertise imply that the pastor or staff member should become a technician or programmer. The key word is the term *operator*. To get the most from the system, pastors and staff members must learn to operate what is present. This is not the same as trying to write or develop software programs. The operator level of computer use means you are able to take a suggested outreach, Sunday School, or stewardship program and put it to work in your church. You can do that because you know your work and understand the program and how it applies. You need to understand the use of the computer and especially word processing and church software so that you can make it work.

Question 2

What are some considerations and guidelines to use if my church is considering a computer purchase (first time or expansion)? Having been in a position to talk to churches considering a purchase of a computer, I can give you a typical opening conversation.

Church representative: "Tell me about your computers."

Sales representative: "I'll be glad to. Could you first tell me a little bit about what you want to do."

The rule that has been suggested for years and violated regularly in making a computer purchase is, "Decide on your software first and then buy the hardware to fit." The part that does the work is the software. If you can't make a software decision, then you really haven't decided what you need a computer to do. In making a software decision you must know what types of work you want to accomplish.

The first step is to think through the types of work you want to do and begin looking for software to do that work. Investigating software is far from easy. A number of companies sell many different church software packages at widely varying prices. A low cost does not guarantee that the software is simple or easy to use. A bargain basement price may be a guarantee that you will have to work hard to master the software and then find when you have learned it that it is severely limited in its application. Some questions to consider when evaluating software include:

- Is the basic screen design easy to read and understand?
- Are help messages available?
- What steps are needed to get a family added?
- How do I get back to an individual record to make a correction?
- How do I make a selection? Can I select on all data fields? How?
- What are the options for sorting a selected list?
- What are the options for producing printouts? Can I design a custom report?
- What are the capabilities for sending data to word processing?
- Does the information kept and general function of the software support the way my church and/or denomination operates?

These questions do not tell you everything about a software package. They do provide some points to use in comparing one system to another. You have several avenues available to evaluate software. These include:

- Look at demonstration diskettes that should show the screens and tell how the software operates.

- In some cases working demonstration copies of the software may be available.
- Talk to other churches using the package. If you receive a bad report, listen carefully to why the report is bad. Would the person giving the report have a hard time using anyone's software or have they really purchased a poor package? The vendor you are dealing with should be able to furnish a list of references.
- Observe a demonstration of the software in operation where you are free to ask questions and say, "Show me how you would . . ."

A final factor in software selection is the reputation of the company itself. Are you dealing with a stable company or an unknown? The field of high technology is notorious for new companies starting up, getting a number of customers, then not being able to continue operation, thus leaving the customers without support.

What about the hardware? Where do I get it? How do I know what to buy? If you have made a decision on software first, then you should already have many hardware answers. The software vendor should have given good recommendations on the best hardware setup. Now, where do you get your hardware? There are at least three distinct choices.

(1) You can buy from a local retail computer dealer. Typically these will be the highest prices, but you may prefer to deal locally.

(2) You can buy by mail. This is normally the way to get the best price. It is also the way to get the least support and assistance in purchasing. If you buy "no name" machines, you will have to depend on your own expertise to know if you are getting the full configuration and specification you need.

(3) You can buy your hardware from your software vendor. There are distinct advantages to this approach. Prices can be compared to other sources. Often software vendors will discount either hardware or software to sell you a full package. If you buy a full package, you can expect to have the system loaded and ready to use on delivery. You also minimize a problem that has plagued the field of computers from the beginning. A common situation is that some problem occurs which gives you an error message on screen. You call the software vendor and are told, "that's a problem with your hardware." You then call the hardware vendor and are told, "that's a problem with your software," and you are in the middle. If everything came from the same source, you should only have to say, "please get it resolved."

In terms of a computer purchase, we have talked about buying software and hardware but are there other considerations? You should think carefully about what you put in your office in terms of function and use. How much computer and how many computers do you need? Who needs to do what at what location? One personal computer with a 40 Mb hard disk and an 80286 processor has the available storage space and processing power to do the work of all except the very large churches. This means that the computer can do the work and store the data, but remember we are talking about one computer with one screen and one keyboard. Can the people who need the computer have access to it when they need to?

Even with the decline in computer prices, buying a system with an 80286 CPU or greater is still an expensive proposition. When the church begins to consider a multiuser system the cost becomes significant. However, given the greater cost of personnel time it can be less expensive to get a computer system to allow a staff to do more rather than continue to add staff and secretaries. The trade off is, "Will the computer system enable the staff to do more?" or, to put it another way, "Will it be effectively used?"

Some considerations in deciding where and how to locate equipment for maximum use are:

● If you put a PC at a desk or in an office it becomes the property of the person. This can lead to difficulties in others having access.

● If the decision is to use a single PC to support the operation, consider having a separate, conveniently located computer room or station that everyone could share.

● If multiple PCs are to be used, what functions are needed on each machine? PCs in staff members' offices or on secretaries' desks that are only needed for word processing do not require the power and disk space of a machine to be used for church record keeping and accounting.

● If a full, multiuser system is to be installed, where will terminals or work stations be located and why? Does every staff member and every secretary need one?

There is one other consideration that may come up in terms of buying a computer or expanding an existing system. Many churches find themselves in a situation where personality becomes a key issue affecting a computer decision. All that can really be said is don't expect a computer to solve personnel problems. If a secretary or staff member is ineffective and cannot do his or her work without a computer, there is no reason to assume that adding one will get the work done. If secretaries and staff are opposed to having computers in the church, they are unlikely to use them effectively. If secretaries and staff do not work well together and cannot schedule time to share equipment, it is not the computer's fault. It is not uncommon to see a church have a computer that is used fifteen hours a week out of forty available hours but has to purchase a second machine because the personnel involved say it's not available when needed. These types of decisions are things the church will have to work out.

Question 3

What's in the future? You may think, *I don't want to buy a new computer or new software every few years.* No one knows what is in the future. The industry has changed and will change. A 1984 book had the following sentence on the back cover: "Here's a single source for up-to-date information on microcomputers."[1] None of the more than one hundred machines mentioned in the book are on the market in 1990. Under the section "Premium Business and Professional Computers," the IBM PC and PC/XT were listed. Two years later, no one would have considered these premium machines. New personal computers have stayed on the market about two years before more powerful models were developed.

No vendor can give any church the guarantee that a particular piece of hardware will last forever. This does not mean that a computer is obsolete within one or two years. A personal example can be used here. The *1984 Buyers Guide* gave a glowing report about a Sanyo 550 series personal computer that had been announced but not yet released. Along with other comments, the review pointed out that the "Sanyo MBC 550 is by far the cheapest of the computers that claim to be compatible with the IBC PC."[2] I purchased a dual floppy disk drive Sanyo 550 in March 1985. The computer has served well but was never 100 percent IBM compatible. Within eighteen months of my purchase, it was possible to buy true compatibles with a hard drive for what I paid for the Sanyo. Today, you can buy a machine with a much more powerful processor and other significant advances for no more than the Sanyo cost me. Is my machine obsolete? In a sense yes it is, but it still does exactly what I purchased it to do. In fact it does more because I added better software than I began with. The manuscript for this book was done on my Sanyo. If a church does a thorough investigation of both hardware and software needs and buys based on sound investigation, then they should not fear new advances.

Some comments should also be made about price. Again no one knows what the future is going to bring. Some reading this book may remember the early 1980s when a Timex Sinclair 1000 was on the market for $49, and a Texas Instruments 99/4A was being sold for $99. These and other low-cost computers turned out to be a fad rather than a revolution. The reality was that if you bought a cheap computer and then added extra memory, disk drives, a monitor, and other things needed to actually do real work, you were going to spend over $1,000. A true full-function computer with a hard drive can be purchased for under $1,800, unless you want to use the 8088 or 8086 chip which is a questionable decision for a church.[3] For a computer with a 40 Mb hard disk, standard memory, VGA monochrome or color monitor, and a full-size keyboard, a price of somewhere around $2,000 to $2,600 is reasonable.

When the new models come out, such as the 80386 processor, then prices are higher on the newer products, but the machines also do more. Computers using the far more advanced 80486 CPU are now on the market. At this point the software industry is behind because software is not capable of doing all the newer processors allow.

Other technology will come as well. Laser printers are already a standard item and will continue to improve. Color printers are available now but not widely used. Compact discs are standard in the recording industry. The technology of compact discs is merging with the technology of computers to allow computers to read data from the discs. The advantage is that incredible amounts of data can be stored on CDs. Boards can be put into PCs to allow a PC to act as a FAX machine. Portable and Laptop computers can be purchased with processors and hard drives that surpass in power what was available only on mini-computers five years ago. Some churches are already using various interfaces with the telephone to send messages to members. Services are available to allow a church to order, on diskettes, census data for their entire community. This data can be read by a PC.

Does any of this change what a church has always done and should continue to do? Churches are the Body of Christ. They are to do the work Jesus did. They are to proclaim the good news of salvation and minister to those in need in the name of Jesus. One of the greatest technological breakthroughs in human history was the printing press. The church used that technology to move forward in one of the most significant times of change in the history of the church. Pastors and church leaders today need to see the computer as a tool that is available at a significant time in history. The computer needs to be used to support, enhance, and enable "the equipping of the saints for the work of service, to the building up of the body of Christ" (Eph. 4:12, NASV). Computers need to be used to obey Jesus' command to, " 'Go out into the highways and along the hedges, and compel them to come in, that my house may be filled' " (Luke 14:23, NASB).

Notes

1. Jerry Willis and Merl Miller, *Computers for Everybody, 1984 Buyers Guide*, (Beaverton, Oreg.: Dilithium Press, 1984).

2. Ibid., 262.

3. The reason the use of an 8088 or 8086 is said to be questionable is that this machine is out-of-date in terms of newer software. If the church already has one, it can produce good work. If the minister is considering a home machine for word processing the 8088 or 8086 is still viable. If a church is considering a purchase, then a machine with an 80286, 80386, or 80486 processor is well worth the extra cost.

Glossary

This section is not intended to be a complete glossary of computer terminology, nor is it intended to provide strict technical definitions. This glossary is provided as a reference to general computer terms as they are used in the text of this book.

Access—To go into information stored in the computer to see a specific record or file.

Backup—A copy of information or programs made to protect against possible machine failure, fire, theft or other loss.

Byte—A basic unit of memory a computer uses to store data. One byte can represent a unique character (letter or number).

Central Processing Unit (CPU)—The part of the computer system that does the work of running programs and processing data.

Church Management Software—Programs designed specifically to do the work of keeping member records, contribution records, attendance, outreach, and so forth.

Data—Information entered into a computer that can be processed or manipulated in some manner. Data could be names, numbers, addresses, birthdays, or practically anything else.

Data Base—(1) A general type of computer program that allows the user to enter any type of data and then have means of manipulating, retrieving, and printing the data. (2) Data base can refer to a file with a great deal of data stored in the file.

Document—A term used in word processing to designate a specific item the user has created that is to be named and saved. A document could be a letter, a memo, a newsletter, a sermon, and so forth.

Documentation—The instructions and manuals that come with a software package and tell the user how to operate the program.

Field—A specific piece of information on a record such as the name, phone number, or birthday on a person's record.

File—A set of information or instructions grouped together and kept by the computer on a disk under a specific name. A file could be all member records or a word processing document. A computer program is normally a collection of files.

Floppy Disk—One type of device for storing information or programs. Floppy disks come in two standard sizes (5.25 inches and 3.5 inches).

Floppy Drive—A device on a computer that allows the user to insert a floppy disk to either take information or programs from the disk or place information or programs on the disk.

Function Key—Special keys on a computer keyboard normally designated F1, F2, F3, and so forth. These keys are given special meaning and uses in different software packages. For example, in word processing a function key might cause text to be underlined or document printed.

Hard Disk—Another possible storage device for computer information and programs. Hard disks are normally found inside the computer unit and keep extremely large amounts of data and programs. Hard disks come in different sizes based on the amount of data that can be stored. A hard disk may be called a fixed disk or hard drive.

Hardware—The physical parts of a computer system such as the monitor, keyboard, computer unit, and printer.

Input—To enter data into the computer or give commands to the computer. The normal means of input is from the keyboard.

Key Stroke(s)—Striking a specific key or series of keys.

Keyboard—The normal input device for a computer. A computer keyboard is similar to a typewriter but with added keys.

Laser Printer—A type of printer that uses a laser to produce high quality copy.

Main Frame—A large type of computer used in colleges, universities, governments, and large businesses. Main frame units require specially trained, full-time, computer personnel.

Matrix Printer (dot matrix)—The most common type of computer printer. Printing is done by a series of wires or pins striking a ribbon and forming the letters or characters.

Microprocessor—An integrated circuit capable of performing all basic data processing operations in one unit.

Mini-Computer—A computer much smaller in size than a main frame but usually larger and with more power than a personal computer. The difference is not always clear and distinct, especially between larger PCs and smaller minis.

Monitor—The TV-like device that displays the work being done from a computer keyboard.

MS-DOS—Microsoft Disk Operating System. The standard operating system for IBM compatible computers.

Network—A means of connecting personal computers through special software and hardware devices so that they may share programs and communicate together.

Operating System—The software that allows a computer to run other programs and do certain functions at the commands of the operator.

Output—Information coming from the processor. Output normally is seen as information being printed, but it could be data sent over a telephone line or a report on the monitor.

PC-DOS—IBM's term for its operating system. MS-DOS and PC-DOS are compatible and will run the same programs.

Personal Computer (PC)—A small computer designed to be operated as a single-user unit.

Printout—Information printed by a computer. Printouts may be in many formats and on many types of paper such as mailing labels, cards, or standard size paper.

Program—A set of instructions written in languages the computer can understand that tell the machine to do specific tasks or jobs.

Programmer—A person who writes computer programs.

RAM (Random Access Memory)—The fast, general-use, working memory of the computer used for operating programs. Random access memory disappears when the system is turned off.

Record(s)—A group of data fields that make up a specific set of information of use to the operator and is kept as a set that can be accessed, for example a member's record.

Software—Computer programs and data.

Spread Sheet—A type of program primarily designed to do mathematical, financial, and statistical functions or other jobs involving numbers. However, spread sheets are not limited to only doing things with numbers.

Word Processing—A type of program that allows the operator to enter words, text, sentences, and so forth and do such functions as edit, move text, create columns, and print the results.

Trademark Acknowledgments

Apple: Apple Computer, Inc.

Atari: Atari, Inc.

Church Information System: The Baptist Sunday School Board

Commodore: Commodore, Inc.

COMPAQ: COMPAQ Computer Corporation

Dell: Dell Computer, Inc.

Electronic Order System: The Baptist Sunday School Board

EveryWord: EveryWord, Inc.

IBM, IBM PC, XT, AT, PS/2: International Business Machines Corporation

Intel: Intel Corporation

Macintosh: Apple Computer, Inc.

MS-DOS: Microsoft Corporation

NewViews: Q. W. Paige

PFS First Choice: Software Publishing Corporation

Phoenix BIOS: Phoenix Technologies, Ltd.

Sanyo MBC 550: Sanyo Business Systems Corporation

SCO-Xenix: Santa Cruz Operation Systems

Tandy: Radio Shack, a Division of Tandy Corporation

Texas Instruments 99/4A: Texas Instruments

Timex Sinclair: Timex Computer Corporation

Unix: Bell Laboratories

WordPerfect Library, WordPerfect 5.1: WordPerfect Corporation